Drake —

Good bless you!

Ted

THE
LIFE-GIVING
CHURCH

The
Life-Giving
Church

TED HAGGARD

Regal

A Division of Gospel Light
Ventura, California, U.S.A.

Published by Regal Books
A Division of Gospel Light
Ventura, California, U.S.A.
Printed in U.S.A.

Cover Design by Kevin Keller
Interior Design by Britt Rocchio
Edited by Karen Kaufman

Library of Congress Cataloging-in-Publication Data
Haggard, Ted.
    The life-giving church / Ted Haggard.
    p. cm.
    ISBN 0-8307-2134-7 (hardcover).
    1. Church management. I. Title.
    BV652.H26 1998   98-27599
    253—dc21   CIP

1 2 3 4 5 6 7 8 9 10 11 12 13 14 15 / 04 03 02 01 00 99 98

Rights for publishing this book in other languages are contracted by Gospel Literature International (GLINT). GLINT also provides technical help for the adaptation, translation and publishing of Bible study resources and books in scores of languages worldwide. For further information, contact GLINT, P.O. Box 4060, Ontario, CA 91761-1003, U.S.A., or the publisher. You may also send e-mail to Glintint@aol.com, or visit their web site at www.glint.org.

DEDICATION

In 1971 Pastor Jon Gilbert was sent by the Home Mission Board of the Southern Baptist Convention to Yorktown, Indiana, to plant a church. While the church was temporarily meeting in the American Legion hall, some of my high school buddies invited me to visit. That visit resulted in a group of us driving with Pastor Jon to Explo '72 in Dallas, Texas, where I accepted Christ as my Savior.

As I continued in high school, my Christian life was shallow and lacked commitment. Then just after I graduated from high school, I was enjoying an exciting weekend night with my friends when my life was suddenly changed.

It was the summer of 1974, and by this time, Jeff Floyd had come to pastor Yorktown Baptist Church. The church had recently built a new building and Pastor Jeff was temporarily living in a trailer nearby until a parsonage was prepared. My buddies and I knew that he was alone in the trailer, so late one night we drove our cars in circles around his trailer until we saw a light come on. Then we drove off only to return in another hour when we were sure the pastor had gone back to bed. After three or four episodes of this mischievous behavior, we unexpectedly saw Pastor Jeff standing in the glow of our headlights. Our cars screeched to a stop. Much to our chagrin, Jeff invited us in. With a gentle spirit and a well-worn Bible, he brought us to our knees on his living room floor. God touched us that night and our lives were forever changed.

Jon Gilbert and Jeff Floyd will probably never be on the cover of *Charisma, Christianity Today* or *Ministries Today* magazines—although I think it would be great if they were. And I doubt that either of them will aspire to writing a book that hundreds of thousands will read—although I think we would all benefit if they did. Nor will either of them pastor a megachurch and enjoy its attending benefits. But they and thousands of pastors like them will pray for us, silently sit with us while we cry, perform our weddings and funerals, answer the phone when we call and faithfully care for our families as well as their own. They will drive vans loaded with our kids to Christian events and bless us in countless other ways.

I think these pastors are heroes. It is because of them that more Americans attend church services every Sunday than attend all of our major sporting events for an entire year combined. As time passes, these pastors accumulate thousands of believers in myriad churches who are living healthy lives because of their godly example: teaching and loving us. Often we don't even acknowledge them with a warm thank-you.

It is to these pastors that we dedicate this book. Jon and Jeff are symbols of the thousands of faithful pastors who come when they are called, sacrifice all for the cause of Christ and unyieldingly service His kingdom.

Thank you, Jon Gilbert. Thank you, Jeff Floyd. We all thank you very much.

TABLE OF CONTENTS

FOREWORD BY C. PETER WAGNER   17
ACKNOWLEDGMENTS   21

SECTION I
FOUNDATIONS FOR
LIFE-GIVING MINISTRY

1. MY FOUNDATION   25
Every church has a personality. The fabric of the New Life
Church story is woven with the values I learned as a boy.
Threaded into those values were my dad's warning to avoid
religious traps and Bethany World Prayer Center's empha-
sis on integrity.

2. CHANGE THE CHURCH? WHY?   39
The Church must be disencumbered from bureaucracy,
inefficiency and gossip to prevent its infant kings and
young Davids from leaving.

3. Our Choice: Life or Death?   49

Adam and Eve had to make a choice between the tree of
life (innocence, the gifts of the Spirit and anointing) and
the tree of the knowledge of good and evil (blame, condemnation and judgment)—so must we.

4. Our Mark: Innocence or Victimization?   63

If we respond to our own sinfulness and to others' sin
with life, then we can enjoy great power and freedom. If,
however, our sin or someone else's sin traps us with a negative response, then we've eaten the wrong tree and have
begun to die.

5. Our Power: Spirit or Flesh?   77

We can't ask for the fruit of the Spirit, receive it through
divine impartation, learn it or create it. It is the product
of His power working through us in normal life situations.

Section II

Philosophy for Life-Giving Ministry

6. Relationships That Empower   93

Life-giving ministry flows through godly relationships,
not corporate structures. And godly relationships—honorably maintained—enable and empower us to fulfill God's
calling.

7. Characteristics That Protect   111

Truth, humility and righteousness are the three characteristics of life-giving churches that provide protective armor
for them.

8. ETIQUETTE THAT SUSTAINS   127
    Long-term relationships cannot survive without manners.
    The kingdom of God suffers when a believer violates deco-
    rum within the Body. Thus, the church world needs proto-
    col as much as any other group.

SECTION III

MINISTRIES OF A
LIFE-GIVING CHURCH

9. MULTIPLICATION OF LIFE: MISSIONS   143
    Life-giving churches don't exist for themselves, but for
    those who don't know life Himself, Christ. The reason
    God gives us His life is to impact our world.

10. IMPARTATION OF LIFE: WORSHIP   159
    By Ross Parsley
    Worship is a physical demonstration of the spiritual reali-
    ties in our hearts. Our physical actions in praise and wor-
    ship reflect the surrendering of our hearts to God.

11. INTEGRATION OF LIFE: FREE MARKET CELLS   173
    With Russ Walker
    There is no way to verify the work of His grace in us if we
    are independent of others; nor is there any way to demon-
    strate godliness to any other than God except through
    interaction with others.

12. DEMONSTRATION OF LIFE: ELDERS   189
    With Lance Coles
    Elders should reflect a Christlike lifestyle that maintains
    the respect and confidence of the people whom they
    serve.

Section IV
Business That Strengthens the Life-Giving Church

13. Church Planting: First Things First 207
With Joseph Thompson
When people show up and get excited about a new church plant, we can easily mistake their enthusiasm as a false signal for God's timing. Many church plants start the same way, and usually lead to hurt feelings and discouraged leaders.

14. Bylaws: Jethro's Request 223
Some structures make ministry easy; others unnecessarily complicate it. These simple Bylaws give people the freedom to minister without providing a license to sin.

FOREWORD

Back in 1985, a young pastor serving on the staff of Bethany World Prayer Center of Baker, Louisiana, which now numbers upwards of 8,000, sensed a clear call from the Lord to launch out and plant a new church in Colorado Springs. With the agreement, the support and the covering of his senior pastor, Larry Stockstill, Ted Haggard moved his family to Colorado Springs and began New Life Church. Colorado Springs was not then the center of evangelical Christianity that it is today, but 1985 is widely regarded as the year that things in the city began to change for the good. One indication of the influence that New Life Church now has in Colorado Springs is the fact that some 6,000 believers show up for worship every Sunday.

When Ted Haggard first arrived in Colorado Springs, then a New Age center that was economically and socially depressed, he had no district superintendent or home mission board to direct his activities and to give him a tried-and-true strategy for planting a new church. Rather than serving under a traditional denomination, Ted Haggard represented a new form of carrying out the life and ministry of the Church, which I have been calling the New Apostolic Reformation.

WHAT IS THE NEW APOSTOLIC REFORMATION?

The New Apostolic Reformation is an extraordinary work of God at the close of the twentieth century, which is, to a significant extent, changing the shape of Protestant Christianity around the world. For almost 500 years, Christian churches have largely functioned within traditional denominational structures of one kind or another. Particularly in the 1990s, but with roots going back for almost a century, new forms and operational procedures are now emerging in areas such as local church government, interchurch relationships, financing, evangelism, missions, prayer, leadership selection and training, the role of supernatural power, worship and other important aspects of church life. Some of these changes are being seen within denominations themselves, but for the most part, they are taking the form of loosely structured apostolic networks. In virtually every region of the world, these new apostolic churches constitute the fastest growing segment of Christianity.

Church planting is built right into the very fabric of new apostolic leaders. Nothing could be more predictable than a staff member of a new apostolic church in our nation and in scores of other nations around the world. But more often than not, the pioneer church planters are largely left on their own to figure out how to get the job done. A strong aversion to bureaucracy, control and standardization of polity have kept most new apostolic leaders from drawing up established principles and procedures for planting new churches and for managing the churches once they are planted.

Ted Haggard has now provided something that every new apostolic church leader has deeply desired—a practical operator's manual, so to speak, for starting and running a church. Many pastors and other church leaders within denominations have also wanted an answer to their question, How are these new fast-growing churches doing it? They will find their answer in *The Life-Giving Church*.

This book provides many practical lessons that are not usually taught in seminary, such as a chapter on etiquette: How do you restore the fallen? How do you take care of guest speakers? How do you hire and fire? Why are good manners so important?

I hope you don't miss the last chapter on Bylaws. I know that very few will read it from beginning to end, but keep in mind that these are new apostolic Bylaws, and therefore quite different from *traditional* church Bylaws. In new apostolic churches, however, it is assumed that the pastor is the *leader of* the church. There is a huge difference between the two mind-sets, and this is one of the first presentations of a model for new apostolic Bylaws provided for church leaders in the form of a book.

I can personally affirm that the advice in *The Life-Giving Church* is good advice. This is not just because I have read and evaluated the book with professional church-growth eyes. Even more, it is because my wife, Doris, and I joined New Life Church when we moved from California to Colorado Springs. Ted Haggard is our pastor. I thought that our wonderful church in California would be hard to replace. But New Life Church has done it!

I have found an incredible presence of the Holy Spirit throughout the life of the church. I have found a passion for the nations of the world that could hardly be surpassed. I have found an incredible love for the community and its people. I have found a spiritual freedom emerging from Pastor Ted's insistence that we live day by day under the tree of life as opposed to the tree of the knowledge of good and evil.

As you read this book, you will see what I mean. If you say, "I want my church to be like that!" you will have made a good decision.

C. Peter Wagner
Fuller Theological Seminary

Acknowledgments

This book reflects a lifetime of exposure to the church world and 13 years of personal experience as a senior pastor. During these years, my staff and I have accumulated ideas and materials from many sources. Our problem has been, though, that the vast majority of ideas within the church world sound good. But only by testing them in the Scriptures and through both personal and observed experiences can we determine which ones actually help.

So we're constantly observing great successes and unfortunately, devastating failures, because of contrasting ministry ideas. That's why I am grateful to the people listed below. They help me think and, as a result, have protected us from many hard lessons. I hope this book will do the same for you.

As you read *The Life-Giving Church,* our prayer is that it will help you avoid painful lessons and ease you into greater effectiveness in His kingdom. And, of course, I trust that it will inoculate you against bad ideas that would inadvertently limit the effectiveness of your ministry.

I believe in learning from others. It's less painful, and I like that. So the following are a few of the organizations and people who have contributed to the strengthening of the local church and have helped form some of the principles presented here:

- My wife, Gayle and our five children, Christy, Marcus, Jonathan, Alex and Elliott. (If these ideas aren't perfected at home, then they don't work at church either.)
- New Life Church staff members: Ross Parsley, Lance Coles and Russ Walker.
- Pastors Roy and Larry Stockstill of Bethany World Prayer Center, Baker, Louisiana.
- Dr. C. Peter and Doris Wagner, Global Harvest Ministries and The World Prayer Center, Colorado Springs, Colorado.
- Tim and Monica Amstutz, Living Word Christian Center, Brooklyn Park, Minnesota.
- Bob Sorge, Sally Morgenthaler and Kent Henry, all great worshipers.
- Martin Nussbaum, New Life Church legal counsel for policies and practices.
- The National Association of Evangelicals, Wheaton, Illinois.

SECTIⓄN I

FOUNDATIⓄNS FOR LIFE-GIVING MINISTRY

1. My Foundation
2. Change the Church? Why?
3. Our Choice: Life or Death?
4. Our Mark: Innocence or Victimization?
5. Our Power: Spirit or Flesh?

This section explains both my personal and the biblical foundation for life-giving ministry. Even though all Christian churches assume that they offer life-giving ministry, the overview provided in this section ensures that we do, indeed, offer life.

1

My Foundation

So it is written: "The first man Adam became a living being"; the last Adam, a life-giving spirit.

[*1 Corinthians 15:45*]

First Impressions

Delphi United Presbyterian Church is where Mom and Dad took me and my three older brothers to church while growing up on a farm in Indiana. My dad was the town veterinarian and owned several businesses and farms. At church, he was a presbyter and enjoyed teaching the high school Sunday School class. Mom did a remarkable job, working at home. She had her home economics degree from Kansas State University in Manhattan, Kansas, the heartland of great food and strong families, and was a professional at making our home and family a work of art. So whether hosting the women's missionary circle, or preparing one of her great meals for our family, Mom was the best. And it was she and Dad who decided the farm and the church were to be the center of our lives.

A few pictures of those years are indelibly imprinted on my mind, and those pictures form the values that shape my view of the local church. I can still see myself sobbing while sitting on the cold tile floor under the table in the basement Sunday School room with the teacher sympathetically pleading with me to come out. I can also see the four of us—Teddy, that's me, the youngest; Timmy, the strongest; Danny, the smartest; and Johnny, the oldest—sitting up straight in our pews with our starched white shirts, dark jackets and clip-on ties.

With our hair perfectly in place, fingernails trimmed and teeth freshly brushed, we stood tall while singing with hymnals in hand. The church seemed huge to me as a little boy, and I was proud of its giant stones, stained-glass windows and towering ceilings. I was awed by the majesty of the pipe organ accompanying the beautifully robed choir, which communicated worship and tidy, Midwestern order.

We each knew that if we poked, punched, whispered, laughed or did anything to draw attention to ourselves, Mom would gently glance at us, which was the first warning. Failure to adhere to the unspoken family rules would lead to the second warning, a gentle touch or soft pinch. But after that, if we solicited even a giggle from another brother that distracted surrounding worshipers from the service, there had better be a loving God in heaven who would help us, because we were going to receive some wholesome encouragement as soon as we got home.

So we didn't. Instead, we always looked forward to the big family meals after church. Sometimes we would go to a little one-room restaurant on the highway that could seat a dozen or so people at a time. Babe, the owner and chef, could make the best fried chicken, mashed potatoes and gravy, corn on the cob and green beans in the world. But most Sundays we would go home to an even better meal prepared by Mom. Sunday meals were always fun and loud, because we all wanted to eat and talk at the same time. I can still see Mom and Dad laughing hard with us during our Sunday dinners.

That's why Delphi Presbyterian Church was such a cornerstone for our family. It was the only time we were consistently formally dressed, starting with Saturday-night baths. And Mom and Dad always made the routine of Sunday worship special. Mom called it the best day of the week. Throughout the week she would count the days until Sunday, which caused all of us to look forward to church.

One time when I was six, everyone was so excited to get home for Sunday dinner that they left me at church. It's a childhood picture I hope I'll never forget. Little Teddy Haggard standing on the church lawn crying with family friends volunteering to drive me all the way to the Haggard farm. Then, when Daddy's Oldsmobile sped around the corner, I could see a look of relief on Mom and Dad's faces. But as the car approached, I could also see my three brothers laughing and pointing at me from the backseat. I was so embarrassed and angry that I jumped into the backseat with my brothers and tried to teach them a lesson by pounding on them.

They just held me and kept laughing at me as I struggled—just what good, big, mean brothers are supposed to do.

These were my first impressions of what a church should be. Our family never considered not going to church. I don't remember that the church service itself was ever anything spectacular and, as I think about it, I don't know that we went because of the services. Instead, we went because we were Christians. Certainly, we never thought of the church as a place for entertainment, or required the church to keep us happy. Rather, it was a major focus of our lives because of the decisions Mom and Dad made about the kind of people they wanted us to associate with and the kind of people they wanted us to become.

Years later when the Lord gave me the opportunity to pastor New Life, I was not particularly interested in building the church on events, entertainment or the most popular movement within the Body at the time. I enjoy those things very much, but I have built New Life on the Word and worship, full of life and power; and I've intentionally structured it to be a great place for parents to raise their children and to graciously mature together as a family. That idea probably came from Mom and Dad's unwavering consistency at Delphi United Presbyterian Church.

Another group of believers in Delphi that significantly impacted my impression of church, and thus the values of New Life Church, were the Dunkers. They were actually Old German Baptist Brethren, but most called them Amish. Like the Amish, they lived simple, rural lifestyles without electricity in their homes and used horses and buggies for transportation.

I was vividly aware of the Dunkers because they traveled to and from town on the road in front of our house. The largest Dunker family, the Royers, would stop from time to time to visit with Mom and Dad. Daddy was their veterinarian and felt very protective of their community because they were completely nonviolent. I remember hearing Dad on the phone telling people that it was our responsibility to protect them so they would have a safe place to farm and raise their families. We were probably as close to the Royers as any non-Dunker family could be. Living near them and knowing them gave me an opportunity to see their humility and sincere faith.

One night a group of drunken high school boys went out to the Royer farm after a football game and began breaking watermelons—the produce that provided the majority of their annual

---

[THE DUNKERS] WOULD NEVER ARGUE OVER MATERIAL POSSESSIONS, NEVER JUDGE ANOTHER OR EVER KNOWINGLY CAUSE ANOTHER TO SIN....THEIR HOMES WERE SIMPLE, THEIR CLOTHING PLAIN AND THEIR SPEECH SOFT AND KIND.

---

income. While the boys were yelling and cussing in the field, the light of a glowing lantern began flickering in an upstairs bedroom of the farmhouse. From the field the boys could see the light being carried down the stairs and then out onto the front porch. Then, as the light approached them through the darkness, the boys were ready for a fight. Instead, Mr. Royer told the boys they could have all the melons they desired, but that the melons they were breaking were not his best. He offered to lead them to the best field and give them as many as they wanted.

The boys were embarrassed and respectfully apologized before leaving. Mr. Royer invited them in for a glass of lemonade—he said they needed it. But the boys declined, trying to soak in their vivid lesson on Christian character. The Royers influenced many people. Instead of preaching with words, they communicated by living well. They would never argue over material possessions, never judge another or ever knowingly cause another to sin. That's why their homes were simple, their clothing plain and their speech soft and kind.

The Dunkers loved the Bible, and actually practiced the Scriptures. They would never dream of resisting an evil man, rebelling against authority or flaunting anything that might stir

---

BEING A CHRISTIAN MEANS...WE STOP STRUGGLING AGAINST ONE ANOTHER IN ORDER TO GAIN THE WISDOM TO WORK TOGETHER IN HARMONY AND TRUST.

---

envy in another's heart. They believed that heaven was their home. Alcoholism, sexually transmitted diseases, divorce, violence and betrayal were unheard of in their community. The Dunkers were models of godly character and conviction for me.

So when I think of a Christian community, I think of the honesty, the generosity and the adherence to Scripture of the Royer family. I would never think of causing others to have to lock their cars, homes or businesses because of my presence. Being a Christian means that the reality of heaven affects every area of our lives, and that we stop struggling against one another in order to gain the wisdom to work together in harmony and trust. These are values I believe all Christians can embrace. Rural cultures don't produce these values, holy hearts do. And Jesus' holiness is available to all of us, no matter where we live—that's what should be evident in our churches.

In Delphi, I remember the back doors of businesses being left unlocked because someone might need something. Daddy used to go into businesses after hours to pick up an item and leave the money and a note on the cash register so the owner would know exactly what he had purchased. Stealing was never a thought. To take something you hadn't earned was shameful. The fabric of our community was woven with trust, honesty and a meaningful handshake. Caring for each other's children and humbly sacrificing for another person's good was the norm, not the exception.

As I write these first impressions of church and Christian people, I realize things couldn't have been as ideal as I remember them. I'm 41 now and know better. However, I do think it's great that these were the memories from the eyes of little Teddy Haggard. I want my kids to have memories just as wholesome. It makes adult life easier. That's why we need good churches.

TRUTH VERSUS RELIGIOUS INSTITUTIONS

Then, when I was in the seventh grade, our world began to change. Daddy's back started to bother him, making it impossible for him to work. Even though his friends tried to help, Dad's pain was so intense that he had to lie on a hard wooden surface without moving, thus we began selling farms and businesses. As the laughter in our home transitioned into caution, Dad saw Billy Graham on television and, for the first time in his life, heard about being born again.

After praying with Billy Graham, Dad went to talk with our pastor who told him that the term "born again" was irrelevant to our modern culture and didn't have any contemporary application. Our pastor warned Dad not to expose our family or his Sunday School class to anyone who believed in being born again.

Even though various people within the community offered to help our family, our financial condition worsened. Dad couldn't stand the thought of borrowing from people in our community, so in the dichotomy of his spiritual renewal and horrible back pain, he and Mom decided to move us to a larger community where they could build a small animal practice that would be easier on Dad's back.

When we moved, Dad found a Presbyterian church that was evangelical, where the pastor understood being born again. But because of his previous experience, Dad was compelled to read and trust his own Bible. While we were settling into our new church home, Dad read about being filled with the Holy Spirit. He asked our new pastor about it and was told not to pursue this experience because it might lead him into fanaticism.

Then, while praying about some of the Scriptures, Dad had a powerful encounter with the Holy Spirit. But because our new pastor had discouraged his seeking this wonderful experience, Dad began to doubt the spiritual integrity of our new church as well...so, we moved on.

Eventually Dad started associating with a group of believers who emphasized the gifts and the power of God's Holy Spirit, a major cultural move for our family. But while worshiping with this group, Dad discovered the Scriptures about deliverance. Because of some old negative patterns that had been deeply rooted in the Haggard family, Dad was very interested in personal deliverance. When he asked his new friends about it, they said Christians never need deliverance, only sanctification. They discouraged him from associating with anyone who believed that Christians could be candidates for deliverance. But Dad and I and some other family members did receive our much-needed deliverance from generations of bondage. Unfortunately, once again, people connected with institutional religion had attempted to thwart our family's growth in the Scriptures and in the power of God.

MY PASTORAL CALL

Therefore, when God called me into pastoral ministry, I was concerned about how Dad would respond. I was home from college after my freshman year as a telecommunications major with a minor in journalism. It was late, and I was by myself in the kitchen, pouring a bowl of cereal when God spoke into my spirit and called me. I was totally surprised.

I paused, smiled and told the Lord I wanted to serve Him. But before I mentioned this to anyone, especially my parents, I asked the Lord to assure me by using others to confirm His calling on my life. I felt as though He consented, so I went into the living room to watch TV and eat Cheerios.

The next morning I received a letter from Curry Juneau, my Sunday School teacher at the church I attended while away at college. Curry wrote that he had been asked by another church to become its senior pastor, and that he would accept the position if I would agree to join him as the youth pastor. I grinned as I read the letter. *Confirmation number one.*

Later that same day Pastor Jeff Floyd, one of the pastors eulogized in the acknowledgments of this book, dropped by the house. He had come to ask if I planned to be in church on Sunday. When I said yes, Jeff was pleased because he said the deacons had voted to license me into the ministry so I could officially begin preparations to be a pastor. They had never spoken to me about this, nor had I hinted at any interest. But Jeff smiled broadly as he told me what they had already decided to do. *Confirmation number two.*

Then that evening, Owen Crankshaw, one of my buddies from high school, came by to pick me up to go out for some fun. As we drove, Owen asked me why I was a telecommunications major when I was going to be a pastor. *Confirmation number three.*

That did it! Pastoral work had never been a subject with my friends before. And yet, after one quick encounter with the Holy Spirit in the kitchen over a bowl of cereal, it seemed everyone knew more than I did about my calling.

But I was cautious about telling Dad that God had spoken to me about becoming a pastor because three respected pastors had given him advice that was contrary to Scripture. Even though I had received three supernatural confirmations, I knew I would not violate my dad's counsel. In my mind I kept hearing him say, *Most traditional churches are worldly institutions that appease God's people and keep them from knowing the Scriptures or the power of God.* Dad no longer trusted pastors to be godly men of integrity, and now I wanted to be one.

The next day I was working in Dad's office and decided to tell him what had happened to me. When I told him, he dropped his head to think, looked up at me, and said he believed God had indeed called me. Then he cautioned: "If worldly church systems or politics ever begin to drain God's life out of you, you must get out quickly. Don't let others kill it." I gave him my word and he gave me his blessing. *Confirmation number four.*

The next Sunday I was licensed at Yorktown Baptist Church and returned to school as a sophomore. Upon my return I switched my major to Biblical Literature with a Christian Education minor, and began working with Curry Juneau at Phoenix Avenue Baptist Church. As I was finishing my bachelor's degree, Phoenix Avenue ordained me and hired me to be an interim pastor for a short time before graduation.

LOCAL CHURCHES WITH A GLOBAL VISION

As graduation approached, I was hired by World Missions for Jesus, a West German missions organization, to become their American representative. World Missions worked exclusively to assist the believers behind the Iron Curtain and in Third World socialistic countries. The risks believers were taking to assist other believers suffering under Communist dictatorships gave me personal insight into the universal Body of Christ, the importance of Christians working in harmony together, and the tragic results that are inevitable whenever Christians separate themselves from one another.

After one and a half years with World Missions, I became the American vice president, which was more administration than I liked. So I resigned from World Missions and joined the ministry team at Bethany Baptist Church, which is now Bethany World Prayer Center in Baker, Louisiana. During the five years at Bethany, my wife, Gayle, and I learned many of the principles for a life-giving church that are in this book:

- Rest.
- Keep your word.
- Don't think more highly of yourself than you ought.
- Churches are to care for others.
- Strong leadership combined with consistency, humility and honesty builds healthy churches.
- Churches are best when not swayed by Christian movements.
- No secrets.

COLORADO SPRINGS

After working with Bethany for five years, Gayle and I thought we would serve there all of our lives. But while on vacation in Colorado Springs visiting Gayle's family, I took a pup tent, a gallon of water, Scripture cassettes and my Bible to the back of Pikes Peak to pray and fast for three days. On that trip, God spoke to me about Colorado Springs and called me to pastor there.

Not long after my arrival in Colorado Springs, during times of praying and fasting, I saw four things:

1. A stadium full of men worshiping God (There were no children or women, but huge numbers of men worshiping God.);
2. A place where people could pray and fast without any distractions;

3. People coming from all over the world to pray for the lost in a world prayer center containing a huge globe;
4. A church where people could freely worship God and study the Scriptures with no strings attached. A hassle-free life-giving church.

After I saw these things in my heart, I believed that God let me see them for intercessory prayer, so I began asking God to bring them to pass. I did not dream that the Lord would actually use me to bring these visions to pass. In the case of the men in stadiums, I haven't had any direct involvement. In the other three, I have had direct involvement:

- The first vision was fulfilled when Coach Bill McCartney received the same idea about 10 years later as he was driving near Colorado Springs. That ministry is Promise Keepers.
- The second vision is Praise Mountain, a prayer and fasting center in Florissant, Colorado that started in 1987.
- The third vision is The World Prayer Center in Colorado Springs.
- The fourth vision is New Life Church.

When Gayle and I came to Colorado Springs in August of 1984, we had been blessed with positive church experiences. Neither of us had ever been involved with a church split, a mishandled moral failure, broken or wounded spirits because of betrayal or deception, or any other common abuses. Because of our history, we knew God had given us great models for ministry. We also knew that if we could just pastor the way we had seen others pastor, we could successfully serve people for many years.

On the first Sunday in January of 1985, New Life Church was birthed with a handful of people in the basement of our recently purchased home. Five months later we moved into our first public space—a little auditorium that sat 200 people with a small room for a nursery and children's ministry.

In May of 1986 we moved down the street to another office building. We reconstructed the inside of the building into a 650-seat auditorium with room for a few classrooms and offices. In 1987, Paul and Geri Fix from Florissant, Colorado gave the church a 70-acre field as a seed toward Praise Mountain, a prayer and fasting center. The church bought two adjacent pieces of property, which resulted in a beautiful 110-acre facility where people pray and fast to this day.

Again in May of 1988, the congregation moved into a larger storefront that was constructed into a 1,500-seat auditorium with a small youth chapel, 12 classrooms and a small office space. That space, like the others before, was quickly filled to capacity, but we couldn't find a space in the city large enough to hold the expanding congregation. It was time to buy land and build.

But because of our strong missions philosophy and our determination not to be wasteful or ostentatious, the church bought land in the county that had to be annexed into the city before construction could proceed. In 1991, New Life Church purchased 35 rural acres on Highway 83 and constructed a simple concrete structure. Our new building had an auditorium that would seat as many as 4,000 with limited classroom and office space. The first service was held Christmas night, December 25, 1991, and since that time, attendance has steadily grown.

Recently we added some additional classroom space to help serve the more than 6,000 members that regularly attend. And, because of our emphasis on missions, the church gave more than $1,000,000 to missions last year (1997). We pray that this kind of giving will continue to increase.

Every church has its own personality and culture. And that personality and culture is composed of the gifts, calling, experiences and personalities of its leadership team and congregation. That's why the value of life-giving churches starts for me in

Delphi, Indiana, with the Presbyterians and the Dunkers. The values learned there, my dad's warning to avoid religious structures and to trust the Scriptures, and Bethany World Prayer Center's emphasis on integrity were fundamental to my personal development, and thus, the foundations of a life-giving church. These elements convinced me that church could and should be simple and effective.

I used to think we were somewhat unique; then I learned that life-giving churches all around the world have discovered how to practice freedom, trust, spiritual sensitivity and honesty in a simple format. In fact, innovative life-giving churches are the fastest growing churches in the world. The negative realities of the "god business" causes me to cling to the simplicity of the life-giving church. Certainly, not all life-giving churches are the same as New Life, many are more established and are of various sizes, but all of them emphasize the power of God, the integrity of the Scriptures and the life available in Christ.

2

CHANGE THE CHURCH? WHY?

EACH ONE SHOULD USE WHATEVER GIFT
HE HAS RECEIVED TO SERVE OTHERS,
FAITHFULLY ADMINISTERING GOD'S
GRACE IN ITS VARIOUS FORMS.

[*1 Peter 4:10*]

Something Is Wrong

New Life Church attracts people who love God but don't necessarily like the church world very much. I can relate. Sometimes I'm like that. I love the Bible, seek the manifestations of the Holy Spirit, enjoy the diversity of the Body and look forward to His Second Coming. Believers make me smile. Prayer is a delight, spiritual warfare is exhilarating and serving others is deeply satisfying. I am thrilled when I think of a good cell group. I like studying the Bible, going on Christian retreats and participating in powerful worship services. They are fun to me because they give me life.

But when most people think of church, they don't think of the life-giving experience that comes from knowing Christ;

TOO OFTEN CHURCHES MAKE NICE PEOPLE
MEAN, HAPPY PEOPLE SAD AND INNOVATIVE
PEOPLE WANT TO PULL THEIR HAIR OUT.

instead they often think of excessive introspection, irrelevant sermons and offerings. Baptisms, weddings and funerals are the only purpose of church for many. And most people draw security from knowing Grandma goes to church. But when thinking of church, few people smile. No one ever says, "I want to have a great party at my house this Friday, so I'm going to invite a group of pastors and church elders." Nope. Doesn't happen. Why? Because too often churches make nice people mean, happy people sad and innovative people want to pull their hair out. Something is wrong on the main street of traditional church structures.

TRANSITIONING CHURCH STRUCTURES TO MOBILIZE MINISTRY

The November 1996 issue of *Christianity Today* profiled 50 people, age 40 or younger, who have demonstrated leadership potential for the next generation of evangelicalism. I am one of those 50. I found it interesting that only 9 of us minister primarily through local church structures. Some of the reasons are obvious: one is a congressman and others are journalists, musicians, educators and professional athletes. But based on the discussions we had when we met at the 1997 National Association of Evangelicals convention, the rest discovered that even though they love their local churches and feel a part of the local Body, they cannot adequately minister through the local church structure. And they are right.

However, the Lord seems to be transitioning the structures He is using to mobilize Christian ministry. Many of us closely associated with local churches are rapidly embracing changes driven by the emerging megachurches and servant ministries. One indicator of this change is that seminaries, our traditional training system for Christian leaders, are not training the leaders of many of our most successful churches or successful servant ministries. Focus on the Family was founded and is prospering under the leadership of Dr. James Dobson, a child psychologist; Promise Keepers was founded and is being directed by Bill McCartney, a football coach.

I don't intend to comment here on the benefits or consequences of the evolving sources of our Christian leadership. But it is so notable that new technical terms are being developed to describe the emerging systems. Renowned missiologist, Dr. C. Peter Wagner, the Conservative Congregationalist from Fuller

Seminary, is regularly writing and speaking about the "new apostolic reformation." Dr. Wagner has accurately recognized the changes as so dramatic that they are creating an actual reformation within the Body of Christ. Without question, we are improving the way we administrate churches and improving the way churches relate to one another.

Dr. Wagner's new book *The New Apostolic Churches* is the most recent publication describing churches that have a powerful ministry of spiritual life and the ministry relationships that emerge around them. This book documents the transformation that is occurring in the way the church administrates ministry.

As I have already mentioned, these transitions are affecting the way churches relate to one another. Several years ago I wrote *Primary Purpose* about the new ways coalitions of churches are working together to promote more aggressive conversion growth in their cities. As a follow-up book, Jack Hayford and I coauthored *Loving Your City into the Kingdom* with Bill Bright, Ed Silvoso, George Otis, Jr. and others to explain how churches can work together to affect their entire city.

Obviously, the Holy Spirit is birthing this dramatic change. The public is seeking out churches that minister life and servant ministries that strategically advance Christ's kingdom. Thus, rapid changes are taking place in existing organizations that desire to grow, and new organizations are birthing from innovation and creativity.

We seldom look to traditional church hierarchies to teach us how to do church anymore. Instead, we look to those on the cutting edge, the thoughtful innovators who are creative and spiritually daring with proven successes. Rick Warren teaches us how to integrate people into our churches, Tommy Barnett teaches us how to illustrate sermons, and Bill Hybels teaches us to consider the seeker's point of view. We don't look to these people for our theological underpinnings, but we are experimenting with ways to communicate a proven gospel message within a rapidly changing culture. So Pentecostals freely receive from Southern Baptist Warren, Baptists unhesitatingly learn from Assembly of God Barnett, and charismatics drink fresh water from evangelical Hybels.

PRESERVING OUR DAVIDS AND INFANT KINGS

Because of improved communication within the Body of Christ, we can find those who know how to most effectively minister life and learn from them. Our entrepreneurs and innovators are rising to the surface, and when they do, we hear about them. That's why I was so fascinated with the 50 people *Christianity Today* chose. They are certainly a promising group, and no one knows which of these will actually make a positive contribution to the growth of evangelicalism.

But, as *Christianity Today* implied, many were not on the list because they are currently unnoticed shepherds. Many of these Davids are in local churches trying to find the mystery of true ministry while serving as youth pastors, music ministers, assistant pastors, cell leaders or volunteers. They love the purpose of the church, but my concern is that when the church bogs down in gossip and inefficiency, they will go where the water flows more freely—outside the local church.

Young Davids want structures that facilitate relationships which are conduits for His living water...the bread of life...the tree of life—that's what future leaders are looking for. But if true life is secondary to a well-intentioned but top-heavy bureaucratic structure that appears political, corrupt or hurts people, then our Davids will graciously excuse themselves. Even the world seems to have caught on to the need to disencumber from the oppressive weight of bureaucracy. The May 14, 1998 headline for *USA Today* reads, "Start-up Davids Don't Fear Goliaths" and the subtitle reads, "Big Can Mean Clumsy, Bureaucratic."

Stimulating greater opportunity within our local churches for our Davids of every age is the reason this book was written. Our future will be brighter when our Davids have a positive experience within their local church structures rather than, like so many other infant kings, being poisoned before they ever approach notable service.

Considering the young Davids, I can't help but think of Bill Gates's book *The Road Ahead*, which emphasizes the necessity of building a corporate atmosphere that attracts and retains the brightest and the best of the business—the entrepreneur. In his book, Gates says that the greatest threat to Microsoft is not NCR, Hewlett Packard, Ford Electronics or IBM, but some college student in a dormitory somewhere playing on his laptop computer, a David. Gates maintains that these Davids are learning what the major corporations already know, but are developing better ideas than paid researchers and developers usually generate.

His concern is that these innovators will get out of school, go to work for Microsoft for a few years until they branch off and start a competing organization that is highly focused in a particular field. That new organization, driven with the creative innocence of the young David, will probably provide a better product at a better price than Microsoft, the large established corporation.

So Gates is taking strong action now. Microsoft's foresight requires it to provide a healthy corporate structure that is not threatened by or passively hostile toward the entrepreneurs, but rather embraces its Davids, causing the entrepreneurs to want to stay within Microsoft. Then, Microsoft will become stronger because of a corporate environment that values the changes birthed by creative innovators. Bill Gates wants the Davids of the microelectronics business to stay, just as we want the Davids of the Body of Christ to be productive within our local churches, not driven from them.

Most young Davids within the Christian world start with an innocent heart before God and a trusting attitude toward churches. They love His life and are innocent before Him. But when they discover cumbersome systems and unnecessary processes that don't contribute to effective ministry, these disillusioned Davids quickly decide they can do more elsewhere. Therefore, our local churches may unnecessarily be losing some of our brightest and best future leaders.

It's no wonder that while we have more money, buildings, books, seminars, seminaries and support groups than ever, 80 percent of our North American churches have either plateaued or are declining. While the Body of Christ is growing three times faster than the population growth rate globally, why hasn't the North American church experienced any net growth in more than 20 years? I think one reason has something to do with how our Davids are being treated within our local church structures. Fortunately, we are changing.

This book offers four sections of information about the life-giving church:

- First is the foundation of life-giving ministry in contrast to ministry that appears godly but doesn't offer life.
- The second is the philosophy, which is vitally important to transitioning from a corporate, highly structured mentality into a dynamic, relational mentality that creates healthy ministry.
- The third discusses some of the ministries of the life-giving church. These are neither simple programs nor departments, but rather tracks that allow apostles, prophets, evangelists, pastors and teachers to enable people within the local church in their ministries.
- Then the fourth section discusses the business structures of the life-giving church, emphasizing how the corporate can serve the spiritual functions of the Body.

Too often church structures restrain godliness and inadvertently provide a voice for ungodliness. We've all grimaced when our structures have unnecessarily given platform to the whiners, manipulators and controllers within the Body, while our strongest innovators gently begin moving toward the door because they don't need to tolerate unnecessary and unproductive systems.

LOCAL CHURCH STRUCTURES TOO OFTEN

STEAL OUR INNOCENCE AND PRODUCE

BONDAGE, SLOWLY DRAINING US OF THE

VERY SPIRITUAL LIFE AND JOY WE ARE

SUPPOSED TO MINISTER TO OTHERS.

We have a paradox. The message of the gospel provides spiritual freedom, but our local church structures too often steal our innocence and produce bondage, slowly draining us of the very spiritual life and joy we are supposed to minister to others. Eventually we become like our predecessors: whitewashed tombs looking good on the outside but powerless and maybe even deadly on the inside.

There is no reason to allow these repressive, encumbering systems to continue to drive the church. What are we protecting? Small bastions of a culture that were squeezed out of mainstream society years ago? Our local churches can be spiritual power-houses of effective ministry *to people*. They should be stable, but not so stable that they are dead. Therefore, our churches must provide simple structures that are tracks for effective ministry rather than restrictive barriers. In the midst of America's spiral away from its Judeo-Christian foundation, God is preparing strong leaders with creative dreams and aspirations for the next generation of local churches to reverse this negative trend.

Attracting and retaining our future leaders within existing local church structures will require some risks as we rearrange the ways we minister with and to the congregation. Certainly, we need the necessary checks and balances to prevent abuse. But we must also recognize that those with the greatest potential require the freedom to test their own wings in order to either fly or fall. If we protect them too much from falling, that same overprotection may keep them from flying. Then we're stuck with more status quo and no net growth in plateaued local churches. We can't afford this any longer. Thus, the transition to *The Life-Giving Church*.

3

Our Choice: Life or Death?

And the Lord God made all kinds of trees grow out of the ground—trees that were pleasing to the eye and good for food. In the middle of the garden were the tree of life and the tree of the knowledge of good and evil....And the Lord God commanded the man, "You are free to eat from any tree in the garden; but you must not eat from the tree of the knowledge of good and evil, for when you eat of it you will surely die."

[*Genesis 2:9,16,17*]

MANY FAITHS,
ONE LIFE-GIVING SPIRIT

Mrs. Morgan has been enjoying the Body of Christ from the same pew of St. Peters practically every Sunday for more than 30 years. The slope in the wood grain eternally marks the exact location from which this faithful church secretary observes weddings, funerals, baptisms and boys fidgeting in their seats. For years she has been watching people come and go, children grow up and marry, and their parents age. From her pew she watches widows grieve the departure of their spouses and children's choirs sing special Christmas songs. Mrs. Morgan faithfully teaches her Sunday School class from the quarterly. At times the church has been healthy and growing with the strength of young men and an atmosphere created by bustling young families. Other times the church has felt tired and solemn, but Mrs. Morgan has never wavered. She loves her church.

Just a few minutes drive from St. Peters is another church of the same denomination. Even though the theology is the same and the people are from the same neighborhood, some even from the same families, the church feels different—its atmosphere is the opposite. For some mysterious reason, people fight easily in that church. They are contentious, defensive and often demanding. Mrs. Morgan has never mentioned anything negative regarding this "sister" church, but when asked, with great sensitivity she graciously changes the subject.

The contrasts between the two churches are evident, despite the fact that the signs in front of their buildings and their listings in the yellow pages indicate that they are of the same faith. But they aren't. The spiritual climate is too different, even though they believe the same creed and read from the same Bible. It is that difference that people notice but can't identify.

This subtle contrast in spirit must be understood in order to build a life-giving church.

When we talk about a life-giving church, we all understand that the life of God is available through faith in the Lord Jesus Christ. By His sacrifice, we have access to the Father, and it is the empowering Holy Spirit who indwells all believers as a deposit

---

IN THIS WORLD OF BLINDED EYES, DULL EARS AND HARDENED HEARTS, THE LIFE OF GOD ISN'T IMPARTED ACCORDING TO FORMULAS...BUT RATHER BY DYNAMIC RELATIONSHIPS.

---

guaranteeing our inheritance in Him. So all churches that believe Jesus is the only solution to our sin problem and that the Bible breathes His revelation into our hearts and minds should be life-giving. Theoretically, all of them are life-giving.

But in this world of blinded eyes, dull ears and hardened hearts, the life of God isn't imparted according to formulas, biblical or not, but rather by dynamic relationships. Most churches that believe the fundamentals of the faith are truly life-giving, but unfortunately, others believe the same things and are deadly. Why?

CREATION AND EDEN

The first two stories in the Bible give us the foundation for our relationship with God and the basis upon which we interpret the balance of Scripture. The Creation account teaches us, among many other things, that God *is*, He is big, and He created everything. No way to avoid it, He's in charge. The account of Adam and Eve in the Garden of Eden gives us insight into the major choice Adam and Eve had to make. They could have obeyed God and continued to enjoy the benefits symbolized by the tree of life, or disobeyed God and died because of the consequences of partaking of the tree of the knowledge of good and evil. This account, for the purpose of our study, provides us with a metaphor that is a picture which helps us see the choice we have to make between those same two trees. And, as in the case of Adam and Eve, one tree gives us life while the other oozes death.

Even though I believe the Eden account is literal, it also provides a figurative lesson for us. As we all know, the Old Testament is full of types and shadows that can be used to strengthen our Christian lives. When we choose the tree of life, we are choosing the life that God offers all of us through Jesus, His Son. The tree of life is a picture of walking and talking with God, living in His provision, protection, fellowship, friendship and lordship. It's a picture of living life full of His Spirit, and having a clean conscience—innocence. But innocence is quickly destroyed when we choose the forbidden, the tree of the knowledge of good and evil. When we choose the tree of the knowledge of good and evil, it brings death.

George Washington Carver, one of our greatest American heroes, exemplified living in the tree of life. Because he was the son of slave parents and raised in abject poverty, he could have been bitter and angry. But he chose not to let the knowledge of good and evil infect his spirit and poison his heart and life. As a result, he said, "I will never let another man ruin my life by making me hate him." Consequently, his brilliant mind was not limited by a bitter spirit, which released him to become one of the greatest inventors in American history.

By choosing the tree of life, George Washington Carver was able to maintain the vitality of the Holy Spirit in his heart and freely minister life to others. If he would have misunderstood and chosen to live according to the knowledge of good and evil, he and those within his influence would have been poisoned by the injustices of his day and would have died spiritually. This is the difference between living according to the tree of life (see Gen. 3:22) and responding according to the tree of the knowledge of good and evil (see Gen. 2:17).

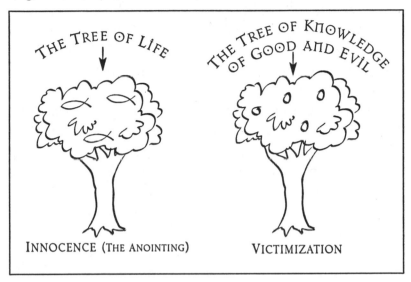

THE TREE OF LIFE

THE TREE OF KNOWLEDGE OF GOOD AND EVIL

INNOCENCE (THE ANOINTING)   VICTIMIZATION

In this chapter I am going to compare the tree of life to the tree of the knowledge of good and evil. Chapter 4 will focus on the attitudes that emanate from these two trees—innocence from one and victimization from the other. Then, chapter 5 will show how these attitudes result in the fruits and gifts of the Spirit or in demonic opportunity, both at individual and church levels.

Now the serpent was more crafty than any of the wild animals the Lord God had made. He said to the woman, "Did God really say, 'You must not eat from any tree in the garden'?"

The woman said to the serpent, "We may eat fruit from the trees in the garden, but God did say, 'You must not eat fruit from the tree that is in the middle of the garden, and you must not touch it, or you will die.'"

"You will not surely die," the serpent said to the woman. "For God knows that when you eat of it your eyes will be opened, and you will be like God, knowing good and evil" (Gen. 3:1-5).

In the opening verses of Genesis 3, we hear the serpent's cunning when he asks, "Did God really say?" This same question, is still the question the serpent asks us today to steal God's plan.

And, like too many of our discussions with the serpent, Eve's dialogue quickly digressed from a simple question about the content of God's Word to a direct contradiction of His Word. When the serpent said, "You will not surely die," he was no longer simply questioning the Word of God, but saying that it was wrong, and offering bait that appealed, oddly enough, to Eve's love for God.

Notice that when the serpent was appealing to Eve to participate in the knowledge of good and evil, he did not directly encourage her to rebel, become her own person, find herself, do her own thing or go her own direction. Instead, he offered her the knowledge of good and evil that would "open her eyes" and make her more "like God." Satan appealed to Eve's love for God and her desire to be like Him. The serpent appealed to her godliness to cause her to abandon the life God had given her and enter into the knowledge of good and evil that had an appearance of godliness but in reality was void of His life.

When the woman saw that the fruit of the tree was good for food and pleasing to the eye, and also desirable for gaining wisdom, she took some and ate it. She also gave some to her husband, who was with her, and he ate it. Then the eyes of both of them were opened, and they realized they were naked; so they sewed fig leaves together and made coverings for themselves (Gen. 3:6,7).

When I was a little boy my mother would sit me on her lap and read Bible storybooks to me that included the story of Adam and Eve. Throughout the years the pictures in these storybooks have been similar, and I think they have influenced the way we read the actual biblical account.

I vividly remember the picture of Adam standing behind a bush and Eve with long hair eating an apple. Because of that picture, every time I read Genesis 3, without thinking I would read "tree of knowledge of good and evil" as "apple tree." Whether this was a literal tree or not, no one knows. I still tend toward a literal interpretation. However, we must not neglect that the point here is consuming "knowledge of good and evil," not a piece of fruit.

I can understand why artists draw apple trees to portray this scene. The woman saw that the fruit of the tree was good for food and pleasing to the eye. With that sentence alone, it could have been an apple, orange, pear or peach tree. But when the Bible says that the tree of knowledge of good and evil had fruit that was desirable for gaining wisdom, it is obviously talking about more than fruit. The fruit that Eve partook could have actually been knowledge. Thus, for our purposes in contrasting the two trees, the tree of the knowledge of good and evil is a worldview, a system of thought, a set of ideas or values that we wrongly think will "open our eyes" and make us "more like God."

Without a doubt, different knowledge produces different outcomes. As medical students study, their eyes are opened to medical realities and, as a result, they are able to assist us with our physical bodies. Trained car mechanics have their eyes opened to the principles that make a car function properly, and the effect is that they know more about cars and trucks than the average person. Some brilliant minds understand the theories associated with Communism, and when they come into power a very different economic and social outcome surfaces than when others with brilliant minds who respect individuals and believe in free markets come into political power.

Knowledge always produces fruit of some kind. The fruit from the tree of the knowledge of good and evil was pleasant to consume and looked fine, and truly was desirable because it appeared to be "wisdom," but consuming this wisdom wasn't as positive as Eve believed it would be. She thought it would open her eyes and make her more like God. She trusted her own misguided judgment instead of trusting God's Word. As a result, she shared the knowledge of good and evil with her husband and their eyes were opened, and both of them were poisoned and began to die.

But the Bible says that they ate the fruit, and the pictures in Mom's storybook showed them eating apples. To eat something means to consume it, ingest it or devour it. Eating means that we take something that is outside ourselves and absorb it into our bodies or lives, to utilize it or take it for our own use. When we read our Bibles, we sometimes refer to it as "eating the Word." When we watch a video, read a book, listen to a teacher or engage in a lively discussion, we are eating knowledge, and that knowledge changes the way we see our world.

Just as the serpent promised, when Adam and Eve ate the knowledge of good and evil, their eyes were indeed opened and they realized they were naked. No doubt about it, they were indeed naked, and always had been. It was never an issue before, but now, with the knowledge of good and evil in their lives, it became a point of shame, and the Lord knew it would affect them that way; that's why he didn't want them to know it.

In Genesis 2:25 the Bible says that "The man and his wife were both naked, and they felt no shame." But in Genesis 3:7, after their eyes were opened because they consumed the knowledge of good and evil, the Bible says "they realized they were naked, so they sewed fig leaves together," in an inept attempt to cover themselves. In other words, they were ashamed of themselves and wanted to cover up. Their innocence was gone. Death had subtly entered through an errant attempt to "be more like God."

Then the man and his wife heard the sound of the Lord God as he was walking in the garden in the cool of the day, and they hid from the Lord God among the trees of the garden. But the Lord God called to the man, "Where are you?"

He answered, "I heard you in the garden, and I was afraid because I was naked; so I hid."

And he said, "Who told you that you were naked? Have you eaten from the tree that I commanded you not to eat from?" (Gen. 3:8-11).

HEAVEN'S SEARCH AND RESCUE TEAM: THE FATHER, SON AND HOLY SPIRIT

God in His sovereignty had to have known that neither Adam nor Eve had the capacity for an open, transparent, childlike relationship with Him any longer. They chose to reject His instructions, but He still came to find them. Here we have the beginning of God's search for disobedient, high-minded, self-reliant humankind. God did not shield Himself or isolate Himself from them. His holiness did not reject them, but rather His heart seemed to long for them. That's why He came looking for them, just as He does today.

God searching for wayward humanity in the garden is the reason most life-giving churches are missions-oriented, outreach-focused churches. God intentionally came to find Adam and Eve even though they sinned. When Jesus confirmed in John 15:16, "You did not choose me, but I chose you and appointed you to go and bear fruit—fruit that will last," He was confirming one more time that He searches for lost humankind.

God's attitude toward fallen humanity is clearly displayed in Philippians 2 where Paul describes Jesus coming as a servant to rescue humanity. Jesus says it Himself in Matthew 20:28 when He turned traditional authority structures upside down by saying, "Just as the Son of Man did not come to be served, but to serve, and to give his life as a ransom for many." Timothy repeats His heart again in 1 Timothy 2:3,4 where he writes, "This is good, and pleases God our Savior, who wants all men to be saved and to come to a knowledge of the truth."

As is our condition today, it was humankind that was hiding from God. Adam says that he was hiding because he was naked, and God doesn't dispute that fact. But there is a tone of hurt in God's voice, I think, when He says, "Who told you that you were naked?" And then the logical conclusion, "Have you eaten from the tree that I commanded you not to eat from?"

[WHEN] MY CHILDREN SHIELD THEIR

HEARTS FROM ME...I SEEK THEM OUT

AND TRY TO GET THEM TO TALK TO ME...

SO SHAME NEVER BOXES THEM INTO

ISOLATION FROM OTHERS.

Gayle and I have five perfect children, as you might imagine— four of whom are boys. On more than one occasion Gayle and I have been sitting in our living room with friends while our three youngest boys were supposed to be taking baths, only to have them come running down the stairs completely naked. Everyone always laughs as these little men dash through the house with their uncovered little bodies being hotly pursued by their embarrassed mother. It's all right because it's innocent. They're children.

On the other hand, sometimes I notice that my children shield their hearts from me. They hide. When that happens, I seek them out and try to get them to talk to me. Usually, something has happened that has placed a barrier between us, or maybe between them and everyone else. It's my responsibility as

their father to coach them in living an honorable life so shame
never boxes them into isolation from others.

I believe that's why God came looking for Adam and Eve. He
knew they had filled themselves with knowledge of good and evil
in their attempt to be more like Him. They had allowed the first
ungodly stronghold in the human race to enter their lives in their
ignoble pursuit of God. But they pursued Him according to what
appeared to be "good" and "pleasing" and "desirable." Their pursuit didn't appear to be bad, painful or repulsive, but it was. It was
a way of thinking that led to a set of poisonous conclusions.

Throughout the Old and New Testaments, the Holy Spirit
clearly requires godly people to change their ways of thinking.
The knowledge of good and evil is so deceptive and subtle, if we
don't guard His life in our hearts by obeying His Word, we can
become quickly deceived and find ourselves separated from life,
which always has the same result: victimization. We either blame
ourselves for everything going wrong, or we blame another. In
Adam's case, he blamed Eve.

> The man said, "The woman you put here with me—she
> gave me some fruit from the tree, and I ate it."
>
> Then the Lord God said to the woman, "What is this
> you have done?"
>
> The woman said, "The serpent deceived me, and I ate"
> (Gen. 3:12,13).

THE KNOWLEDGE OF GOOD AND EVIL: THE TREE THAT CREATES SPIRITUAL ORPHANS

Here we see the second evidence that death was entering their
hearts: They were blaming each other because they were not
content with simple obedience and the life it afforded them. In

Paul's first letter to the church in Corinth, he discusses the war of ideas that must be fought. It's a battle of values, thoughts, principles and systems that either clears the way to find His life, or subtly begins to enslave us with a deceptive knowledge of good and evil that produces death in our spirits.

These systems of ideas are so strong and controlling that Paul calls them strongholds that must be demolished. But once we understand that life does not come from expertise in good and evil, but rather in revelation of life and death, then the mystery of genuine life is within our grasp and we may find the kingdom of God. Unless we understand the flow of life in contrast to the mechanics of death, we have little hope of ever leading a life-giving church.

> For though we live in the world, we do not wage war as the world does. The weapons we fight with are not the weapons of the world. On the contrary, they have divine power to demolish strongholds. We demolish arguments and every pretension that sets itself up against the knowledge of God, and we take captive every thought to make it obedient to Christ (2 Cor. 10:3-5).

It's the knowledge of good and evil that gives us a value system which tells us that we are naked and should hide from God. It's also the knowledge of good and evil that gives us the parameters with which to judge another so we can say "Eve did it," and "The snake did it." Disobedience gave Adam and Eve the ability to know, blame and judge, which led to God having to clearly articulate the consequences of their search for godliness in disobedience. The serpent was cursed (see Gen. 3:14,15), and both the man and the woman had the consequences of their disobedience listed for them by God (see vv. 16-19).

Then God displays, in type, that their own garments won't cover their sin because no blood was involved. So as another act of mercy, He covers them with garments of skin to remind us all that it is only through the blood of another that our shame can be covered. Then, at the end of the chapter, God limits humankind's access to the tree of life, so they won't live forever on their own without finding life in Christ Himself. Humankind no longer has access to life on their own, but now by knowing life Himself, Jesus, we can find eternal life.

> And the Lord God said, "The man has now become like one of us, knowing good and evil. He must not be allowed to reach out his hand and take also from the tree of life and eat, and live forever." So the Lord God banished him from the Garden of Eden to work the ground from which he had been taken. After he drove the man out, he placed on the east side of the Garden of Eden cherubim and a flaming sword flashing back and forth to guard the way to the tree of life (Gen. 3:22-24).

I love to travel all around the world, taking teams of intercessors to spiritually strategic sites to pray for the outpouring of the Holy Spirit. On those journeys, we've visited the places of worship of every major religion. In these sites, I find sincere people searching for God. Mosques, temples, churches and religious sites are used by millions of people daily, touching the spiritual world. Most of these worshipers pray, read holy books, burn candles, rub beads, give offerings, dip in rivers and pour water over statues in their deep pursuit of a relationship with the Almighty God. Few actually find Him, but they don't realize it because they experience a sense of spiritual fulfillment through the soulish satisfaction that comes from the tree of the knowledge of good and evil.

Most religious people know they have had a spiritual experience because it has enlightened them; it has opened their eyes and they know good and evil. They also know that their spiritual journey has given them satisfaction; it's been "good for food."

And, as with Eve, their spiritual devotion produces a positive change in their lives; it's "pleasing to the eye."

Unfortunately, these characteristics are universal in all religions, including Christianity. Many "Christians," Jewish believers, Islamic worshipers, adherents to Hinduism and Buddhism all enjoy the benefits and the consequences of the tree of the knowledge of good and evil. Only those who have pressed beyond religious practice and have come to know Him, the God of Abraham, Isaac and Israel, through His Son, Jesus, can know God. For it's in knowing Him that the mystery of genuine godliness starts to unfold. And it is, indeed, a relationship that is a narrow path—a path that can only be navigated according to the Scriptures by the Holy Spirit. It's easy, but it requires understanding relationships, not just creeds. That's why, after Genesis 3, the Bible begins telling the stories of God's encounters with people to teach us about Him. He's a person, we're people, and to have His life we must learn to know Him.

4

Our Mark: Innocence or Victimization?

AND HE [JESUS] SAID, "I TELL YOU THE TRUTH,
UNLESS YOU CHANGE AND BECOME LIKE LITTLE
CHILDREN, YOU WILL NEVER ENTER THE KINGDOM
OF HEAVEN. THEREFORE, WHOEVER HUMBLES
HIMSELF LIKE THIS CHILD IS THE GREATEST
IN THE KINGDOM OF HEAVEN."

[*Matthew 18:3,4*]

It's a Heart Attitude

We all love to hear the children sing at Christmas time. I used to wonder why because they usually can't sing very well. They fidget, can't remember the words and are often so enamored with the crowd that they are usually distracted. But those things don't matter. They are cute, innocent, little children and we all love innocence.

In Matthew 19:14 Jesus said, "Let the little children come to me, and do not hinder them, for the kingdom of heaven belongs to such as these." Even David in Psalm 103 advances this idea when he writes, "Praise the Lord, O my soul...who satisfies your desires with good things so that your youth is renewed like the eagle's."

Many times when I see people come to Christ, they have a sinless look on their faces that communicates childlike innocence. They always look clean. Through the years I've noticed that believers who understand living in the tree of life have this same childlike purity about them. I'm convinced that innocence is the by-product of knowing Jesus, and the conduit for His anointing.

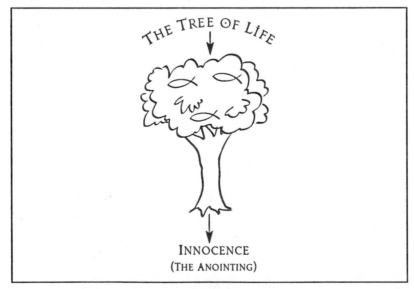

From the lips of children and infants you have ordained praise (Matt. 21:16).

Men such as Billy Graham, T. L. Osborn and John Arnott from Toronto are great examples of the strength of innocence. They have remained untainted throughout years of ministry, which actually disturbs their critics. They respond to criticism with simple honesty, preventing it from hardening their hearts and ruining the anointing.

ONE OF THE GREATEST MARKS OF OUR CHARACTER IS OUR RESPONSE TO SOMEONE ELSE'S SIN.

Women such as Katherine Kuhlman, Ruth Graham and Freda Lindsey are the same way. Even though they are aware of their shortcomings, they have stayed above the seductions of the knowledge of good and evil and have remained free to minister His freedom. Throughout the years, all of these have maintained a simple childlikeness that allows the Holy Spirit to freely flow through them, and God likes that. Like children, they have more fun than most, and that's refreshing.

Two women can be standing outside an abortion clinic holding signs saying "Stop Abortion Now." Even though they are similarly dressed and are protesting the same problem, one may be in the tree of life and the other in the knowledge of good and evil. The difference is the motivation of their hearts.

The tree of life protester is there because of love and compassion for the mother, unborn child and even the father. She wants to try to help those struggling with their pregnancies. In contrast, the tree of knowledge of good and evil protester is there because abortion is evil, those who participate in it are evil, and they must be stopped. The tree of life protester will enjoy a sense of innocence and peace of heart, and the Lord will use her in a special way. She reflects Him. The other protester has fallen into the tree of the knowledge of good and evil and has squarely placed blame. She has identified the victim of her wrath and, in her self-righteousness, has inadvertently fallen into sin. This subtle difference of the heart is one of the most important biblical messages.

One way we can tell if we are enjoying the tree of life or suffering under the consequences of the knowledge of good and evil is our response to sin. Our response to our own sin can only adequately be settled in the life of Christ, but one of the greatest marks of our character is our response to someone else's sin. If we respond to our own sinfulness and to others' sin with life, then we can enjoy great power and freedom. If, however, our sin or someone else's sin traps us with a negative response, then we've eaten the wrong tree and have begun to die.

God warned Adam that eating from the tree of the knowledge of good and evil would kill him, and in Genesis 3 and 4 we see shame in Adam and Eve as they hide from God. Later, we see Cain killing Abel. Their eyes were opened, but they didn't become like God. Instead, they became like the one they chose to obey: The serpent. The accuser.

The serpent has not stopped. He still asks, "Did God really say?" and continues to offer anything that will draw people away from the life Christ offers. For some it's a good, religious life. For others it's good works in the secular world. For others, it's blatant evil. The serpent doesn't care as long as people don't find Christ's empowering life. Then he has accomplished his task of keeping people in darkness so they will spend eternity in hell. Jesus, however, wants people to come to Him and to receive life, knowing that His life is the only way we can live forever.

INNOCENCE

Staying innocent does not mean that we ignore or reject ideals of good and evil. In Genesis 4, God speaks clearly to Cain and explains that if he will do the right thing, then he will be accepted. God is not saying that doing the right thing is the life of God, but He is saying that there is a path to life. He continues in the same paragraph by explaining that sin is crouching at the door of our hearts and that we need to resist sin in order to pursue the will and plan of God.

Some people grow in their understanding of right and wrong from the tree of life and find great insight, wisdom, victory and joy in the stream of Jesus' righteousness. These people have a high view of right and wrong and use it to direct themselves and others toward life. Others, though, base their understanding of right and wrong in the wrong tree. This results in frustration, judgmental attitudes and ultimately death.

Both good and bad people are dead without life. Life comes from Christ alone, and His fruit is righteousness. His righteousness is the only place where we can find absolute right, which is our plumb line for right and wrong. If we don't understand His righteousness, as revealed both in the Scriptures and in our hearts through His Spirit, then any standard of right and wrong is merely subjective to our culture or our personal preferences. If we do, though, use a religious standard for right and wrong outside of Christ's life, we have found the knowledge of good and evil and will unknowingly begin going down the path that leads to death.

This process explains why some good people get so mean being good. We've all heard jokes about church secretaries, deacons' meetings and leaders who "love God" but can't constrain anger, bitterness or other areas of their sinful nature. All of these people have a form of godliness, but many times their attempt to be godly produces such anger and frustration that their actions deny the very power of God they had hoped to represent.

For as the Father has life in himself, so he has granted the Son to have life in himself (John 5:26).

In Galatians 5, the apostle Paul lists for us the acts of the sinful nature (see Gal. 5:19-21) and the fruit of the Spirit (see vv. 22-26). Most who study these two lists think of them as a list of evil things to avoid and a list of good things to do. Not so. Each list is a mirror that helps us see if we are living a spirit-filled life or not. Should our lives fall short, the message of the book of Galatians is to discover the truth of the gospel and be increasingly filled with the Holy Spirit so genuine freedom in Christ can be found (see v. 1).

That's why neither the Old Testament nor the New could simply give us a creed by which to live. It's more personal than that. The Scribes and the Pharisees, the Bible scholars of Jesus' day, didn't come close to understanding. So Jesus told them in John 5:39, "You diligently study the Scriptures because you think that by them you possess eternal life. *These are the Scriptures that testify about me, yet you refuse to come to me to have life*" (italics added).

It seems as though these good people studied the Scriptures diligently and missed the point completely, just as we so often do. They were neither studying the Scriptures nor living their lives in the tree of life, but were studying and living according to the tree of the knowledge of good and evil. That's why Jesus called them whitewashed tombs and vipers (see Matt. 23:27,33). Jesus rebuked the Bible scholars of His day for missing the primary messages of the Scriptures, but He loved the humble worshipers who had childlike hearts.

"I praise you, Father, Lord of heaven and earth, because you have hidden these things from the wise and learned, and revealed them to little children. Yes, Father, for this was your good pleasure" (Matt. 11:25,26).

It's important to understand that Jesus was not speaking against thoughtful examination of the Scriptures. Nor should we construe that God's warning about the knowledge of good and evil could be an exhortation to keep us from studying and gaining knowledge. He was simply emphasizing the necessity of a heart submitted and open to Him. That's why Jesus Himself had to display for us that the Word must be written in our hearts so believers actually become living epistles. We don't just read the Word and believe it, we become it through knowing Him. We're resurrected in His life.

To clarify this, Jesus emphasizes:

- "I am the *bread of life*" (John 6:35,48, italics added).
- "I am the *living bread* that came down from heaven. If anyone eats of this bread, he will live forever. This bread is my flesh, which I will give for the life of the world" (John 6:51, italics added).
- "I tell you the truth, unless you eat the flesh of the Son of Man and drink his blood, you have no life in you. Whoever eats my flesh and drinks my blood has *eternal life*, and I will raise him up at the last day. For my flesh is real food and my blood is real drink. Whoever eats my flesh and drinks my blood remains in me, and I in him. Just as the living Father sent me and I live because of the Father, so the one who feeds on me will live because of me. This is the bread that came down from heaven. Your forefathers ate manna and died, but he who feeds on this bread will live forever" (John 6:53-58, italics added).
- "I am the resurrection and the *life*. He who believes in me will live, even though he dies; and whoever lives and believes in me will never die. Do you believe this?" (John 11:25,26, italics added).
- "I am the way and the truth and the *life*. No one comes to the Father except through me" (John 14:6, italics added).

Jesus' teaching had to transition those who wanted a relationship with God from the tree of the knowledge of good and evil to the tree of life. Because much of Judaism had become a religion of "godly" action instead of a relationship with God, Jesus had to challenge the fundamental way the Scriptures were being applied. So He emphasized that without a relationship with Him, a relationship with the Father was impossible. That's why He said we had to eat His body and drink His blood. Christianity is more than an intellectual assent to the principles of the Bible; it requires actually consuming Him so His life dominates our lives. To gain life takes believing and more, it requires dying and becoming again, in Him. That's why He said He is:

- The Messiah (see John 4:26);
- The Light (see John 9:5);
- The Gate (see John 10:7);
- The Son of God (see John 10:36);
- The Lord (see John 13:13);
- The Way, the Truth, the Life (see John 14:6);
- The Vine (see John 15:1);
- The Alpha and the Omega (see Rev. 1:8,17).

Jesus gives us these metaphors to help us understand that only by knowing Him can we know His life. He is the source of living water (see John 4:10), which gives life (see Ezek. 47; Rev. 2 and 21). Paul communicates the necessity of knowing Him for the Jewish culture by contrasting attempts to be saved through obedience to the law and the assurance of salvation promised through the grace made available by the Cross. Genesis introduces the same principle with our choice between the tree of life, Jesus, and the tree of the knowledge of good and evil.

JOY VERSUS JUDGMENT

On occasion I have appeared to be like a monkey jumping between these two trees. I've been in the tree of life with the joy, innocence and anointing, only to have someone come up and say something critical to me. Immediately, I jumped out of the tree of life into the tree of the knowledge of good and evil and became sinfully defensive. I could feel a cloud of death starting to grow in my heart, and part of me liked the fight. But I was using the knowledge of good and evil to demonstrate how I was right and they were wrong. But in fact, I was right and wrong at the same time. At best, empty victory. I technically won, but I didn't. I started to die. I was right, *dead* right!

Now I've learned, though, when I'm criticized, to remain in the tree of life while responding. The innocence of that response leaves my heart clean and gives my critic a greater opportunity to find the tree of life as well. What a relief! With the tree of life I am still able to respond and explain, but everyone stays clean. That's genuine victory.

When we go to church in the tree of life, we are grateful for the congregation, grateful for the staff, grateful for the leadership, and want to make ourselves available to serve. It's a joy to give, a delight to worship, and easy to pray and fellowship with those around us. But attending church in "the tree of knowledge of good and evil" attitude is quite different: We go because of duty or obligation, not because we draw life from church. When we get there, we attend with a critical eye. So if the pastor, the volume or the temperature isn't correct, a sour spirit starts developing in our hearts. And, if a need surfaces somewhere in the church, rather than helping we criticize.

Bible reading can have the same dynamic. When I read the Bible from the tree of life perspective, joy is always evident. Like a child I submit to the Scriptures and let them speak deeply into my heart. I can always tell when I'm in the tree of life because I want to mark lots of the verses and make prolific notes. But I've had other times when I've read my Bible from the knowledge of good and evil point of view where I read it out of a duty or a goal or an obligation. The struggle of trying to get through a certain number of chapters or trying to read for a certain time period every day can be a source of death.

When I was in high school, I read a chapter from the Bible every night before I went to sleep, no matter where I had been, how late it was, or how tired I was. That was a blessing to me. Since then I have set goals that didn't add fresh life to my spirit but instead became a religious duty and obligation which actually darkened my spirit. If I were trying to read a certain number of chapters, I would find myself resenting long chapters rather than learning from them. Or, if I were trying to read my Bible for a certain time period, I noticed that time seemed to stop. It was hard work. But if I would stay in the tree of life, I found that I read more of the Bible for longer periods of time, using chapter goals or time goals simply as guidelines but never as the end in themselves. If the goal is anything other than Him, it quickly degenerates into religious legalism, which causes us to judge.

Prayer is the same way. "Tree of life" praying is when worship, intimacy, communion with the Father and an easy connection with the Spirit is natural. It's getting into your prayer closet and worshiping and praying until you are done. Tree of knowledge of good and evil praying is different. When you are driven to do it because you ought to do it, it becomes a miserable trap. You get into your prayer closet knowing that you have to pray for a certain period of time or get a certain list covered. It's dry, rote and lacks connection. It's satisfying to a degree, because it makes us feel as though we have done something good. This, however, is not nearly as satisfying as knowing His life.

- The purpose of serving is to reflect the life of God.
- The purpose of Bible reading is to learn the personality of God so His life can freely flow through us.
- The purpose of prayer is fellowship, friendship and communion. In prayer we confront demonic schemes

and commune with God. We engage darkness and grow in the Holy Spirit to become more effective vessels of His life.

However, in the tree of knowledge of good and evil, we mistakenly believe that doing good is an end in itself. It's good to go to church, protest abortion, pray and read our Bibles. It's good to be good. It's satisfying to be good. It looks good, tastes good and feels better than being evil. But goodness is not life unless it is a result of His life.

Living in the tree of life includes constructive discipline that makes us better people. When I pray, I ask God to convict me strongly so I can live in the refreshing of His Spirit and walk in His life. That conviction keeps me clean, and His discipline motivates me toward life.

Childlike innocence has an optimistic view of the future and learns the lessons from the past but doesn't let the failures or negativity of the past dictate our futures. It focuses on learning, growing and developing for a stronger future. It highlights sanctification as a positive process that protects our lives and ministries, and seems to always embrace light. Confession, healthy relationships and willingness to accept responsibility in order to correct a difficulty is inherent in tree of life living. Forgiveness, gratefulness, appreciation with its attending joy and peace allow innocence to reign as we live in the tree of life.

VICTIMIZATION

But the dangerous sword of victimization is birthed when we live according to the knowledge of good and evil. Sometimes victimization convinces us that we can't obey God because of someone else's actions or our personal weaknesses. Adam blamed Eve, Eve blamed the snake and Cain blamed Abel. Displacing responsibility never helps. As soon as we place blame, we are saying that

Jesus is not actually our Lord, but whoever or whatever it is that we are blaming really is.

Adam admitted that Eve was his lord instead of God. He obeyed her voice, not God's. Eve admitted that she allowed the serpent to be her lord instead of God. By Cain killing Abel, Cain let Abel

---

THE TREE OF KNOWLEDGE ALWAYS
MAKES US POINT AT SOMEBODY AND SAY,
"I CAN'T, BECAUSE THEY DIDN'T."
BUT THE TREE OF LIFE SAYS,
"I CAN, NO MATTER WHAT THEY DO."

---

become the lord of his attitudes and actions rather than God. We do the same thing when we blame the economy, deacons, the devil, witchcraft, negative social trends, our parents or our spouses. Whatever or whomever we blame, we place in lordship over us.

We are often more victimized by our own hearts than by what has happened to us.

The tree of knowledge always makes us point at somebody and say, "I can't, because they didn't." But the tree of life says, "I can, no matter what they do." That keeps them from being your lord, consuming your thoughts and controlling your life. The tree of life says, "If someone slaps you on one cheek, turn the other cheek, walk a mile with them, give them your cloak, and kiss them as you invite them to church." That drives demons crazy.

As a matter of fact, it drives people crazy who want to manipulate you into hating them. Some people will actually try to do something bad enough to you to gain control in your life. They will say bad things about you, knowing you will hear about it. If you respond according to the tree of the knowledge of good and evil and are hurt by them, they have, in effect, taken control of you. But if you stay in the innocence of the tree of life, they are frustrated because they can't get into you because you forgive and maintain your freedom.

That same deceptive sword of victimization can cut the other way as well. When it's not cutting against us, dethroning Christ in our hearts, it's causing us to use seemingly good things to cut against others around us. We become convinced that we have achieved some position in God that others haven't achieved; or that we are more obedient, disciplined or blessed. That superior tone will always backfire. Proverbs 16:18 says, "Pride goes before destruction, a haughty spirit before a fall."

For example, if I believe it is godly to read five chapters of the Bible a day, and I successfully read five chapters every day, I'll establish this as the standard for godliness. My knowledge of good and evil tells me that when I read my five chapters a day, God likes me and that I am walking secure in Him. When I meet other people, if they are reading their five chapters a day, then they meet the godly standard. But when I meet people who say they are Christians but are not reading five chapters a day, I somehow make sure they know that they should be reading five chapters a day in order to be a successful Christian. And, until they do that, they will not be as successful as I am. Even though that sounds good, it's deadly.

Victimization produces guilt and insists upon punishment. It provides fertile soil for the serpent to accuse and condemn. It always uses fear and causes people to focus on the past and dread the future. It finds fault, places blame and demands retribution whenever possible. Victimization loves the darkness so it entices us to hide portions of our lives, cover for failure and avoid personal responsibility.

Because victimization uses guilt, it prompts us to make promises that can't be kept, vows that will soon be broken and powerless ideals that cannot be fulfilled. Once broken, failure begins to define our view of ourselves and our relationship with God and others, causing us to lose the joy and peace that Christ intends through His sacrifice.

CHOOSE LIFE

When we choose life, we receive refreshing innocence that is a conduit for His anointing, which manifests by producing the fruit of the Spirit and His gifts. The mark on our lives is either innocence or victimization, and each receives strength from either the Holy Spirit or the darkness of our sinful natures. Life-giving churches freely operating in the gifts and displaying the fruit of the Spirit are what we all desire. The next chapter explains how we can grow in this dimension of His life.

5

OUR POWER: SPIRIT OR FLESH?

HE HAS MADE US COMPETENT AS MINISTERS
OF A NEW COVENANT—NOT OF THE LETTER
BUT OF THE SPIRIT; FOR THE LETTER KILLS,
BUT THE SPIRIT GIVES LIFE.

[*2 Corinthians 3:6*]

BE ON THE ALERT

A young graduate from seminary feels called by God to plant a church. He pursues this call with all his heart, knocking on doors, inviting people and meeting in a school cafeteria. The Lord blesses, and the little fellowship grows. People are saved, baptized, healed, delivered and the fruit and gifts of the Spirit flow beautifully.

Finally, several hundred people are attending regularly, and a permanent meeting place is clearly needed. The first building committee is formed. The members of the committee search for sites prayerfully, but a major split soon develops. Some want to build in the prospering suburbs, where most parishioners live, while others want to establish a place downtown to reach out to a needy community.

People take the debate very personally. One side argues, "We are going to lose people if they have to drive 45 minutes to get to church."

The other side responds, "God calls us to minister to those in need. A church in their neighborhood is the best way to do that."

The young pastor is in the middle, trying not to offend either side. Meanwhile, he finds his prayer life suffering. His chief concern is the next business meeting. He finds himself looking hard at the amount in the offering and wondering how to increase it.

Many churches and pastors start out in innocence with the Spirit of God moving there, but then an issue arises where people start judging and taking sides, and sinful bickering in God's name soon develops. At this point, demons have an opportunity to wreak havoc. On the other hand, this challenge provides an opportunity for a demonstration of the fruit and gifts of the Spirit. The power to choose lies with the pastor and the people.

This chapter will tell how the fruit and gifts of the Spirit increase when believers stay in the tree of life. It will also help you spot the warning signs that demonic opportunity has been allowed. Finally, I will briefly overview some specific issues that can either bring life or death to a church body as a whole.

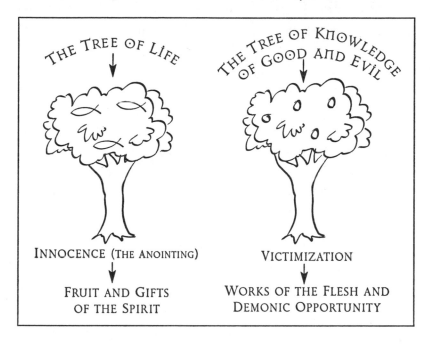

THE TREE OF LIFE

THE TREE OF KNOWLEDGE OF GOOD AND EVIL

INNOCENCE (THE ANOINTING)

VICTIMIZATION

FRUIT AND GIFTS OF THE SPIRIT

WORKS OF THE FLESH AND DEMONIC OPPORTUNITY

Then the angel showed me the river of the water of life, as clear as crystal, flowing from the throne of God and of the Lamb down the middle of the great street of the city. On each side of the river stood *the tree of life*, bearing *twelve crops of fruit*, yielding its fruit every month. And the leaves of the tree are for the healing of the nations (Rev. 22:1,2, italics added).

Bad decisions, regardless of the motivation, produce unintended consequences. If you don't make an effort otherwise, offenses will grow, become cancerous, destroy relationships and infect other people, and potentially the entire church. The Scripture warns about the root of bitterness that pollutes many (see Heb. 12:15).

When we make a decision to stay in the tree of life, any situation can refine our character and make us stronger people of God. Problems won't grasp us and control us and determine our futures. Instead we stay innocent so we can fulfill God's plan. When we stay innocent, the anointing of the Holy Spirit is free to flow.

The first step is to be filled with the Holy Spirit.
When I repented and asked Jesus to come into my heart, the Holy Spirit came into me and made me a new creation (2 Cor. 5:17; Rom. 8:16). The first people to experience this new birth, as we understand it as members of the New Testament Church, were the disciples. In John 20:22, Jesus breathed on them and said, "Receive the Holy Spirit." In that instant the disciples were just like we are as born again believers:

1. They had received the Holy Spirit (see John 20:22).
2. Their names had been written in heaven in the Lamb's Book of Life (see Luke 10:20).
3. They had already established a personal relationship with Jesus because He was with them physically (see Matt., Mark, Luke and John).

But Jesus commanded them to have an additional encounter with the Holy Spirit: "Do not leave Jerusalem, but wait for the gift my Father promised, which you have heard me speak about. For John baptized with water, but in a few days you will be baptized with the Holy Spirit" (Acts 1:4,5). Because they didn't understand the significance of what Jesus was asking them to do, the disciples began talking about Jesus' political takeover of Israel.

So Jesus redirected their attention by saying their role did not necessitate knowing the times and the dates, instead He pointed out that this baptism in the Holy Spirit was of supreme significance. In Acts 1:8, He returns to the subject and describes what will happen to them when they are baptized in the Holy Spirit:

"But you will receive power when the Holy Spirit comes on you; and you will be my witnesses in Jerusalem, and in all Judea and Samaria, and to the ends of the earth."

Because Jesus had already breathed on them and commanded them to receive the Holy Spirit in John 20:22, they already had the Holy Spirit. But Jesus wanted them to wait in Jerusalem for the gift the Father had promised. What gift was He talking about? The disciples already knew Jesus, so we know His relationship with them wasn't the gift. And they already had their names written in the Book of Life, so we know that eternal life wasn't the gift referred to here. In addition, they already had the Holy Spirit working in their lives, so that wasn't the gift of which Jesus was speaking. The only thing they hadn't received was this baptism in the Holy Spirit, which Jesus was comparing to John's baptism in water.

To ensure clarity, Jesus emphasized that the gift the Father had promised could be compared to the water baptism of John. Jesus said, "John baptized with water, but in a few days you will be baptized with the Holy Spirit" (Acts 1:5). The word baptism means to dip, immerse, sprinkle, submerge or dunk. In some cases it means to anoint. So Jesus' meaning was clear. Just as John the Baptist had been dipping, immersing, sprinkling, submerging and dunking people in water, in a few days the disciples were going to be dipped, immersed, sprinkled, submerged and dunked in the Holy Spirit. Just as the baptism of John had an anointing about it that prepared people for the coming of Christ, so the baptism in the Holy Spirit would carry its own anointing of fire.

Acts 2 tells the story that established the Church, as we know it today:

Suddenly a sound like the blowing of a violent wind came from heaven and filled the whole house where they were sitting. They saw what seemed to be tongues of fire that separated and came to rest on each of them. All of them were filled with the Holy Spirit and began to speak in other tongues as the Spirit enabled them...."We (Jews who spoke various languages) hear them declaring the wonders of God in our own tongues!" Amazed and perplexed, they asked one another, "What does this mean?" Some, however, made fun of them and said, "They have had too much wine" (Acts 2:2-4,11-13).

Immediately Peter stood up and began preaching to the crowd and explained, "These men are not drunk, as you suppose" (v. 15). Then he began quoting from Joel 2:28-32 and explained that they had been filled with the Holy Spirit, which was a fulfillment of Jesus' instruction.

"In the last days, God says, I will pour out my Spirit on all people. Your sons and daughters will prophesy, your young men will see visions, your old men will dream dreams. Even on my servants, both men and women, I will pour out my Spirit in those days, and they will prophesy" (Acts 2:17,18).

It had happened. Humankind, fallen from the innocence of the Garden of Eden, had now rediscovered the full measure of life flowing from their hearts toward God. Jesus prophesied it in John 7:38 and 39 when He said, "'Whoever believes in me, as the Scripture has said, streams of living water will flow from within him.' By this he meant the Spirit, whom those who believed in him were later to receive. Up to that time the Spirit had not been given, since Jesus had not yet been glorified."

But now Jesus has been glorified and we have the privilege of being filled with the Holy Spirit. So to have life-giving churches, we must have Spirit-filled people.

In order to maintain a Spirit-led attitude in my own life and church, I pace myself with great care by scheduling my time according to priorities. I have a Bible and prayer plan that is life-giving and refreshing. I enjoy praying and fasting, both alone and from time to

ENCOURAGING SCRIPTURES
ABOUT THE HOLY SPIRIT

I baptize you with water for repentance. But after me will come one who is more powerful than I, whose sandals I am not fit to carry. He will baptize you with the Holy Spirit and with fire (John the Baptist speaking, Matt. 3:11).

If you then, though you are evil, know how to give good gifts to your children, how much more will your Father in heaven give the Holy Spirit to those who ask him! (Jesus speaking, Luke 11:13).

I am going to send you what my Father has promised; but stay in the city until you have been clothed with power from on high (Jesus speaking, Luke 24:49).

And I will ask the Father, and he will give you another Counselor to be with you forever—the Spirit of truth. The world cannot accept him, because it neither sees him nor knows him. But you know him, for he lives with you and will be in you. I will not leave you as orphans; I will come to you (Jesus speaking, John 14:16-18).

But I tell you the truth: It is for your good that I am going away. Unless I go away, the Counselor will not come to you; but if I go, I will send him to you (Jesus speaking, John 16:7).

time with friends. I love praying with people in our church to assist them in being born again, filled with the Holy Spirit, and victorious over the sinful nature and demonic resistance. We are the Church, the only ones who can help others find liberty. And to fulfill our call, we must be filled with the Holy Spirit.

Unfortunately, this experience has been debated so much in the tree of the knowledge of good and evil that most believers think they are filled with the Holy Spirit if they simply believe what they view as the "correct interpretation" about this subject. But the Bible says we will know if we've been filled with the Holy Spirit by our fruit (see Matt. 7:16; John 15:2). The evidence doesn't lie (see Luke 6:43-45). So, if we don't have the fruit, we aren't filled. We will exhibit whatever is in our hearts. So if we are full of the Holy Spirit, we will demonstrate His life like rivers of living water.

The super-megachurches in Asia, Central and South America, and Africa that are experiencing exponential growth all encourage their people in lifestyles that cooperate with the power of the Holy Spirit. None of them are afraid of the person of the Holy Spirit or His manifestations. They understand that the gifts and fruit of the Spirit are vital necessities for the powerful life that Christians require.

Follow the way of love and eagerly desire spiritual gifts, especially the gift of prophecy (1 Cor. 14:1).

The Bible has several lists of the gifts or manifestations of the Holy Spirit's presence in our lives. The following are two of the passages with their references:

Now to each one the manifestation of the Spirit is given for the common good. To one there is given through the Spirit

- the message of wisdom, to another
- the message of knowledge by means of the same Spirit, to another

- faith by the same Spirit, to another
- gifts of healing by that one Spirit, to another
- miraculous powers, to another
- prophecy, to another
- distinguishing between spirits, to another
- speaking in different kinds of tongues, and to still another
- the interpretation of tongues.

All these are the work of one and the same Spirit, and he gives them to each one, just as he determines (1 Cor. 12:7-11).

We have different gifts, according to the grace given us. If a man's gift is...

- prophesying let him use it in proportion to his faith. If it is...
- serving, let him serve; if it is
- teaching, let him teach; if it is
- encouraging, let him encourage; if it is
- contributing to the needs of others, let him give generously; if it is
- leadership, let him govern diligently; if it is
- showing mercy, let him do it cheerfully (Rom. 12:6-8).

Once we are filled with the Holy Spirit and are operating in His gifts, the streams of living water flow naturally. We're to choose the tree of life, live in childlike innocence and seek the gifts of the Holy Spirit. As we enjoy the attending benefits, one of the greatest joys we can experience is the natural outcome of His power in us.

But the fruit of the Spirit is love, joy, peace, patience, kindness, goodness, faithfulness, gentleness and self-control. Against such things there is no law (Gal. 5:22).

The wonderful truth about the fruit of the Spirit is that it is just that, fruit. We can't ask for it, receive it through divine impartation, learn it or create it. It is the result, the effect, the product of His power working through us in normal life situations. And it is always tested.

- Love is tested by our desire to take care of ourselves or those near to us in preference to those who are outside of our own circle of friends.
- Joy is tested when everything goes wrong.
- Peace is tested when we have too much to do.
- Patience is tested when we're in a hurry.
- Kindness is tested when someone needs a firm hand.
- Goodness is tested when we want attention ourselves.
- Faithfulness is tested when loyalty has run out.
- Gentleness is tested when we're feeling harried.
- Self-control is tested when no one is watching.

Unfortunately, some have read lists like this from the tree of the knowledge of good and evil and have attempted to attain these virtues through their own strength, only to fail. Rather than enjoying life and easily producing fruit, they are actually living in death while trying to produce godly fruit—and it doesn't work. The resulting frustration opens the door to the acts of the sinful nature and demonic opportunity, which is the final consequence of choosing the wrong tree.

Throughout the Bible we see supposedly godly people dominated by their old sin natures oftentimes becoming influenced by demonic activity. Even our current generation has been embarrassed by Christian leaders whose personal lives revealed that they didn't know the power of God in a life-giving way and were trapped in ungodliness.

Not only individuals but entire churches and movements can also fall into this rigid, religious trap. Remember the story of

Mrs. Morgan, the church secretary at St. Peter's church, who was faithfully serving in a life-giving church. St. Peter's had a sister church that believed the same creed but didn't enjoy the anointing of the Holy Spirit and thus, had lost its innocence, and neither the fruit nor the gifts were evident within that Body.

———

ONCE WE FALL INTO VICTIMIZATION...IT'S ONLY A MATTER OF TIME BEFORE THE SINFUL NATURE AND THE EVIDENCES OF DEMONIC INVASION BEGIN TO MANIFEST.

———

Once we fall into victimization and lose the childlike freedom that Jesus provides, it's only a matter of time before the sinful nature and the evidences of demonic invasion begin to manifest. Many times we'll try to maintain a clean exterior appearance but in our hearts greed and self-indulgence slowly take root. As time progresses in the knowledge of good and evil, hypocrisy, public positioning, secrecy and at times seeds of blatant wickedness begin to grow. The Bible says in Galatians 5:19-21: "The acts of the sinful nature are obvious: sexual immorality, impurity and debauchery; idolatry and witchcraft; hatred, discord, jealousy, fits of rage, selfish ambition, dissensions, factions and envy; drunkenness, orgies, and the like."

Lists such as this that warn us are common in the Scriptures. Revelation 21:8 says, "But the cowardly, the unbelieving, the vile, the murderers, the sexually immoral, those who practice magic arts, the idolaters and all liars—their place will be in the fiery lake of burning sulfur. This is the second death."

Jesus emphasized the importance of clean living when He said,

"If your hand causes you to sin, cut it off. It is better for you to enter life maimed than with two hands to go into hell, where the fire never goes out...And if your foot causes you to sin, cut it off. It is better for you to enter life crippled than to have two feet and be thrown into hell...And if your eye causes you to sin, pluck it out. It is better for you to enter the kingdom of God with one eye than to have two eyes and be thrown into hell, where 'their worm does not die, and the fire is not quenched'" (Mark 9:43,45,47,48).

How then can we be saved? Only by consuming Jesus as He is found in the Scriptures and being empowered by His Spirit, the Holy Spirit. Every other attempt leads to failure.

GOD'S POWER VERSUS HUMAN GOODNESS

Islam has a well-meaning but harsh religious code that attempts to keep people holy. Because of their attempt to please God, they pray five times a day, wrap their women in black robes and limit exposure to every potential vice. They block the sale of alcohol and pornography. They teach and try to practice many notable disciplines, but haven't found life. Many are angry, bitter religious zealots; others go through the motions but in actuality have given up. They can't do it.

Every other religion is the same. From the Hindu and Buddhist temples to the Jewish synagogues to many Christian churches, we find people learning to live better lives, but finding at best a "knowledge of good and evil" which satisfies to a degree but does not offer the liberating life that transforms hearts.

Last October while in Nepal we observed the sacrifice of chickens and goats to idols. No life. No healing. No power. The worshipers even admitted to us that their gods never answer prayer and the blood of the goats doesn't help them. But they still do it because the knowledge of good and evil satisfies their soulish desire to seek God.

In the same way some Christians recite words, rub beads, pray to statues and give, hoping that God will respond to them. Their religious rituals offer no more life than those of an Islamic, Buddhist or Hindu worshiper. All are worshiping out of the tree of the knowledge of good and evil unless they go beyond the routine and find life Himself, Jesus. To know Him and the power of His resurrection requires openness to His Spirit and a freedom in His life, so His gifts and fruit can freely develop. Then and only then is God's life adequately infused into the worshiper and displayed in genuine ministry.

The apostle Paul said it clearly when he wrote in Romans 8:1-8,12-17, "Therefore, there is now no condemnation for those who are in Christ Jesus, because through Christ Jesus the law of the Spirit of life set me free from the law of sin and death. For what the law was powerless to do in that it was weakened by the sinful nature, God did by sending his own Son in the likeness of sinful man to be a sin offering. And so he condemned sin in sinful man, in order that the righteous requirements of the law might be fully met in us, who do not live according to the sinful nature but according to the Spirit.

"Those who live according to the sinful nature have their minds set on what that nature desires; but those who live in accordance with the Spirit have their minds set on what the Spirit desires. The mind of sinful man is death, but the mind controlled by the Spirit is life and peace; the sinful mind is hostile to God. It does not submit to God's law, nor can it do so. Those controlled by the sinful nature cannot please God.

"Therefore, brothers, we have an obligation—but it is not to the sinful nature, to live according to it. For if you live according to the sinful nature, you will die; but if by the Spirit you put to death the misdeeds of the body, you will live, because those who are led by the Spirit of God are sons of God. For you did not receive a spirit that makes you a slave again to fear, but you received the Spirit of sonship. And by him we cry, 'Abba, Father.'

The Spirit himself testifies with our spirit that we are God's children. Now if we are children, then we are heirs—heirs of God and co-heirs with Christ, if indeed we share in his sufferings in order that we may also share in his glory."

This passage explains why life-giving churches must be saturated in the Word of God and filled with the Spirit. If not, the sinful nature takes over and demonic activity becomes evident. The apostle Paul warned the church at Ephesus not to give the devil a foothold (see Eph. 4:27) before he emphasized to them that their struggle was not with one another but against spiritual forces looking for an opportunity to weaken, and if possible destroy, the church (see Eph. 6:10-18). James repeats this warning when he writes "Submit yourselves, then, to God. Resist the devil, and he will flee from you" (Jas. 4:7).

How do we know when the enemy has been given a place in our lives and our churches? When we see people becoming critical, unsatisfied, beginning to be hypersensitive and harsh in their defense of what they believe is "godly." When I pray for the believers who worship at New Life, I ask God to protect them and keep them in life-giving relationship with Him and with their brothers and sisters in Him. I also pray the Word will stay alive in them and that all demonic forces will be thwarted in their schemes to paralyze Christians.

The enemy is aggressive and powerful, ready to capitalize on every area of weakness. So if we allow religious footholds to begin in our hearts and consequently in our churches, it's only a matter of time before our church will no longer be life-giving but rather dead, regardless of our creed. Therefore, we must be diligent to pursue His life, His innocence, His anointing, His gifts and allow the fruit of His Spirit to freely flow so the kingdom of God is manifested in people's hearts with the accompanying evidence of good works birthed by His Spirit.

Section II

Philosophy for
Life-Giving Ministry

6. Relationships That Empower

7. Characteristics That Protect

8. Etiquette That Sustains

This section provides practical examples of life-giving ministry
that apply to every area of life. With relationships, characteristics and etiquette well understood, nothing can prevent us from
continuing to grow and minister in His life.

6

Relationships
That Empower

Two are better than one, because they have
a good return for their work: If one falls
down, his friend can help him up. But pity
the man who falls and has no one to help
him up! Also, if two lie down together, they
will keep warm. But how can one keep warm
alone? Though one may be overpowered, two
can defend themselves. A cord of three
strands is not quickly broken.

[*Ecclesiastes 4:9-12*]

The Divine Flow of Relationships

Moses knew he couldn't do it alone. He didn't speak well; he knew Pharaoh was the most powerful man in the world; he also knew that Egypt would not release the children of Israel. God strengthened Moses by adding Aaron to Moses' calling. Aaron strengthened Moses, and together, they liberated Israel.

"Relationships are the only thing we take to heaven with us," an old Baptist preacher once said. I've heard businesspeople say that everything they know is subordinated to their people skills. If they can't relate well with people, their ability to provide goods and services to others is greatly hampered. A board member of one of the world's largest corporations told me that people who understand relationships are the ones who enjoy true success.

Some grumble that success is too often based on "who" we know rather than "what" we know. I think it's a fact. Even our eternal destinies are determined by our personal relationships with Christ. If we know Him, we go to heaven. If we don't, we don't.

Several years ago I read a little booklet by John Osteen, a pastor in Houston, Texas, entitled *The Divine Flow.* This booklet explains how the Holy Spirit creates a divine flow between people's hearts that, if responded to properly, can supernaturally build relationships. He explains that we can often determine God's perfect plan in building purposeful relationships for His kingdom by learning to respond to the divine flow in our hearts.

Pastor Osteen develops the idea further by applying it to our relationships within the Church. He says we should learn to sense God's divine flow toward other people because it may mean we are supposed to work together in a meaningful way in His kingdom. Sometimes this divine flow feels like a welling up of love, or a desire to devote special attention toward a particular person. Other times the divine flow causes us to have an unusual interest in another person.

Several years ago I was asked to speak for the Godly Men's Conference at Oral Roberts University. During the meeting I noticed a divine flow in my heart toward the worship leader, Ross Parsley, who is now a trusted friend and the worship pastor here at New Life. In that same series of meetings, a student working outside the chapel, Russ Walker, caught my attention. He is now my associate who oversees our small group ministry.

The flow can happen both ways. Another student who attended the conference, John Bolin, had a miracle happen in his heart that touched his spirit. He felt a sense of being connected with me, even though we hadn't met. Now, years later, he and his wife, Sarah, have moved to Colorado Springs and serve as our youth pastors. Joseph Thompson, another associate pastor, read my book *Primary Purpose*, and experienced a powerful sense of connectedness with me. As a result, he and his family are now here powerfully serving in God's work.

Life-giving ministry flows through godly relationships, not corporate structures. Corporate structures give us order and define our roles, but relationships empower us. It's the relationships with family members, elders, staff members, community leaders, the press and volunteers that are the core of life-giving ministries. When God creates supernatural relationships to make us more effective—if they are honorably maintained—they can empower and enable us to fulfill God's calling.

The following are seven sets of relationships that empower successful life-giving ministry. All of these relationships funnel people toward eternal life through Christ, and the more levels we understand, the more effective our ministries. As you read the list, notice that each additional level of relationships has increased breadth of impact, and each level requires its own revelation. These relationships are the way God strengthens us to fulfill His calling. He wants us to understand and flow in relationships that empower us to do what He wants done.

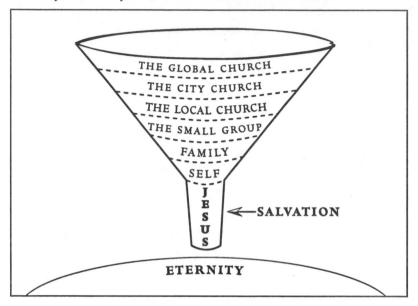

Relationship #1: Jesus
Result: Salvation

> "I am the good shepherd; I know my sheep and my sheep know me—just as the Father knows me and I know the Father—and I lay down my life for the sheep" (John 10:14,15).

In order to have a life-giving ministry, we must be confident that we have been born again into a vital relationship with Christ. In this generation of "easy-believism," many people think they have been born again, when in fact, they have not. Jesus said in Matthew 7:21-23, "Not everyone who says to me, 'Lord, Lord,' will enter the kingdom of heaven, but only he who does the will of my Father who is in heaven. Many will say to me on that day, 'Lord, Lord, did we not prophesy in your name, and in your name drive out demons and perform many miracles?' Then I will tell them plainly, 'I never knew you. Away from me, you evildoers!'"

When Jesus gave us the Great Commission to reach the world, He said, "Go and make *disciples* of all nations, *baptizing them* in the name of the Father and of the Son and of the Holy Spirit, and *teaching them* to obey everything I have commanded you" (Matt. 28:19,20, italics added). Note that He did not say, "Go into all the world and have people repeat a salvation prayer."

Because many misread the Great Commission, millions of people believe they are born again, but they neither know Him nor live lives that have been transformed by the power of the Holy Spirit (see 2 Cor. 5:17). Philippians 2:12 says, "Therefore, my dear friends, as you have always obeyed—not only in my presence, but now much more in my absence—continue to work out your salvation with fear and trembling, for it is God who works in you to will and to act according to his good purpose."

Prayer, expressing our heart's repentance, is without a doubt the way we are all born again. But being born again is only the doorway to the ultimate purpose of knowing Him. If we guarantee people that they have begun a relationship with Christ and have received eternal life just because they repeated a prayer, we might be assuming too much. There is no way for any of us to know the condition of another person's heart. So when repeating or reading a prayer, some do begin their relationship with Christ, but others don't. The horrific reality might be that if they were just repeating words and we tell them they are now guaranteed eternal life, we might be giving them false assurance that could contribute to their going to hell. We as life givers point the way and direct people to Christ, but each individual must faithfully pursue his or her own relationship with Christ and work out his or her own salvation with fear and trembling.

In 1972 I prayed to receive Christ along with thousands of other high school students at Explo '72 in Dallas, Texas. In that prayer, I expressed my love for Christ and my desire to have Him live in me. Upon returning home, I started going to church and reading my Bible, but my internal life did not change. I didn't stop any of my normal non-Christian high school student activities. I was fully living in the world but involved in the Bible and church. Then, after my senior year of high school, my pastor led me in a prayer to "sell out," to commit my entire life to Christ. After that prayer, my life dramatically changed—evidence of becoming a new creation.

So, when did I become a Christian? I tell people I got saved at Explo '72, but something makes me wonder if Explo '72 didn't begin a process that led to a genuine conversion experience two years later. I don't know with assurance, and I don't want to endlessly discuss the salvation process here. But I do want to emphasize that in order to have life-giving churches, we need to know, with absolute assurance and evidence in our hearts and lifestyles, that we are securely and verifiably in a dynamic relationship with Christ.

Jesus is the cornerstone of the Church. Our relationship with Him is foundational to every other relationship we have; it empowers us to assist others. Once our relationship with Him is secure and growing, then He is able to create and maintain all of our other relationships, which will create healthy ministry. He is the life giver for all life-giving relationships. He is the foundation of every life-giving church.

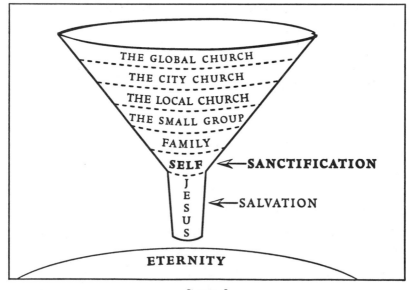

Relationship #2: Self
Result: Sanctification

> May God himself, the God of peace, sanctify you through and
> through. May your whole spirit, soul and body be kept blame-
> less at the coming of our Lord Jesus Christ (1 Thess. 5:23).

Every growing Christian knows the war that can sometimes develop
between our spirits, our souls (sometimes defined as our minds,
wills and emotions) and our bodies. When we come to Christ, our
spirit becomes a new creation, but the soulish portions of our lives
and bodies are still just as they were before conversion. That is why
Christian growth over time is required to settle internal conflicts so
we can safely minister to others. The reason the Bible lists qualifications for eldership and standards for Christian leaders is not because
of God's struggle in dealing with sinful humanity, but because certain lifestyles give us credibility in the hearts of other people.
Personal sanctification validates His message through us. Therefore,
if we attempt to minister without internalizing His life to some
degree of comfort, we can horribly embarrass the Body of Christ.

First Thessalonians directly addresses this issue by saying, "It
is God's will that you should be sanctified: that you should avoid
sexual immorality; that each of you should learn to control his
own body in a way that is holy and honorable, not in passionate
lust like the heathen, who do not know God; and that in this
matter no one should wrong his brother or take advantage of
him. The Lord will punish men for all such sins, as we have
already told you and warned you. For God did not call us to be
impure, but to live a holy life" (4:3-7).

Only time, trial and error, failing and trying again, thinking,
praying, talking and sharing with others in the Body can work
sanctification into our lives.

Jesus emphasized the role of the Word in the process of sanctification in His John 17:17 prayer, "Sanctify them by the truth;
your word is truth."

Peter emphasized the role of the Spirit when he said that we have been chosen "according to the foreknowledge of God the Father, through the sanctifying work of the Spirit, for obedience to Jesus Christ and sprinkling by his blood: Grace and peace be yours in abundance" (1 Pet. 1:2).

The book of Hebrews emphasizes the role of the relationships within the Body of Christ (see 10:19-39) by explaining how God's righteousness is integrated into every area of our lives. Within the heart of this discussion, Hebrews 10:25 says, "Let us not give up meeting together, as some are in the habit of doing, but let us encourage one another—and all the more as you see the Day approaching."

As we grow in Christ, He establishes His lordship over our bodies, minds, wills and emotions, so our lives become increasingly productive. If these internal conflicts are not settled, we may become spiritual time bombs, potentially destructive to His kingdom. Thus, in order to build a life-giving church, we must consistently allow the Word, the Spirit and healthy relationships within the church to keep our lives in harmony so His life-giving Spirit can flow unhindered through us.

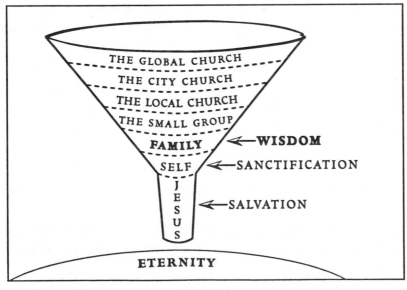

Relationship #3: Your Family
Result: Wisdom

> He [an overseer] must manage his own family well and see
> that his children obey him with proper respect. (If anyone
> does not know how to manage his own family, how can
> he take care of God's church?) (1 Tim. 3:4,5).

Even though the traditional family is under siege by western culture, the relational dynamics of a traditional family are invaluable and must be preserved within our Christian community. A husband and a wife in relationship with their children have a greater potential for success because the home is the primary place God designed to train all of us in positive, healthy relationships.

Every relational dynamic we need can be developed within the school of the home. For example, Paul says in Ephesians 5:22-33 that the relationship between the husband and the wife is to model the relationship that exists between Christ and the Church. This dynamic provides the insights into God's love for His people, servant-style leadership, our love for one another, compassion, caring, intimacy, respect and giving. Biblical references to intimacy, acceptance, boundaries, affection and rejection, and other significant emotions and attitudes reflect God's love for His people and His desire for intimacy with them. These characteristics are most powerfully integrated into our lives through our marriages.

Gayle and I have five children. Before our children came along I thought the role of parents was to help their children grow up. I have discovered that this is only partially true. I now know that the role of children is to force their parents to grow up. You can't be selfish and successfully raise children.

Children teach us how to live for others and how to relate to various ages. Babies don't care about income, titles or influence. They demand our attention and respect. If we withhold it, they'll punish us. And these lessons apply to every child in relationships with siblings as well.

In our home, Christy is 16, Marcus is 15, Jonathan is 10, Alex is 7 and Elliott is 5. When any of them fight, they must settle their differences without leaving. Divorces are not allowed. No one can leave home while fighting. Everyone must realize that in order to play happily, we all have to adjust to and understand one another. And we have to know who is in charge. If any of us becomes selfish, the home becomes unhappy for everyone. If a job needs to be done, it is accomplished with greatest ease when we all work together.

Family dynamics provide the wisdom for successfully leading a healthy church. The home should spawn rules of decency, kindness, respect, honor and contentment—all necessary for a life-giving church. The balance of law and grace, autocratic rule and group dynamics, giving justice and the positive role of discipline are principles we all must learn in order to have a healthy home and church.

If the discriminating insights required to maintain long-term relationships are not learned at home, divorce or hurt will follow. The same holds true for the church, and the potential for separation, broken relationships and wounded hearts increases. I am not saying that our families must be perfect to function normally in a life-giving church. I am saying, though, that the wisdom learned

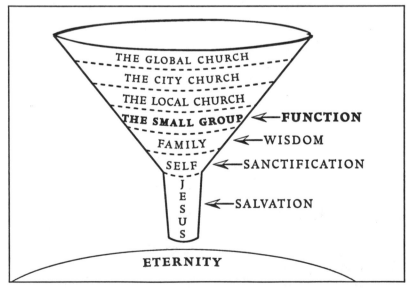

through the family dynamic is invaluable to understanding how to build and maintain the relationships required to have a long-term, life-giving church.

Relationship #4: The Small Group
Result: Function

As iron sharpens iron, so one man sharpens another (Prov. 27:17).

Every successful church has some method for helping people to meet and form dynamic friendships within the Body. Some

---

ANY DEMON, NO MATTER HOW WEAK,

CAN PENETRATE A CORPORATE STRUCTURE.

BUT NO DEMON, NO MATTER HOW STRONG,

CAN PENETRATE A GENUINE FRIENDSHIP.

---

churches use cells or other small groups to accomplish this goal, while others use Sunday School classes. But every successful pastor knows that friendships within the Body are what hold the church together and cause it to function.

To emphasize my strong belief in friendships, I often say, "Any demon, no matter how weak, can penetrate a corporate structure. But no demon, no matter how strong, can penetrate a genuine friendship." At New Life, 392 small groups meet every week. Because of those groups, new friendships are constantly forming, helping our church family to stay strong and healthy.

Many of the great Bible heroes understood genuine friendships. Ruth 1:16 says, "Don't urge me to leave you or to turn back from you. Where you go I will go, and where you stay I will stay. Your people will be my people and your God my God." First Samuel 20:17 is one of many verses that talk about the way David and Jonathan strengthened one another. Here the Bible says, "Jonathan had David reaffirm his oath out of love for him, because he loved him as he loved himself."

The Gospels make note of several of the friendships Jesus maintained. Some just wanted to serve the Lord, while others were His disciples. Matthew 27:55 says, "Many women were there, watching from a distance. They had followed Jesus from Galilee to care for his needs." In the Garden of Gethsemane, Jesus wanted His closest friends, Peter, James and John, with Him. He drew strength from His friends, just as we do (see Matt. 26:36-46).

Strong healthy friendships make all of us more secure, positive, productive and effective than we could ever be alone. They produce an upward synergy that activates strength. Paul was very frank about his relationships with the church at Philippi when he wrote in Philippians 1, "I thank my God every time I remember you. In all my prayers for all of you, I always pray with joy because of your partnership in the gospel from the first day until now,...It is right for me to feel this way about all of you, since I have you in my heart;...God can testify how I long for all of you with the affection of Christ Jesus. And this is my prayer: that your love may abound more and more in knowledge and depth of insight" (vv. 3-5,7-9). Paul understood the importance of the divine flow and genuine friendships.

These friendships teach us how to function in the calling God has given us. In small groups we refine the righteousness God is working into our lives in a practical way. In small groups we learn how to apply the lessons we have learned in our walk with Christ to our family relationships. In small groups we incorporate life lessons into our public lives. Honest friendships keep us from being deceived or diluted into hypocrisy. My friends sharpen me and help me see the blind spots, making me a more capable person. Small groups are the strength of the local church. They keep it from evolving into a simple religious organization, and keep it functioning as a life-giving Body linked together with positive relationships.

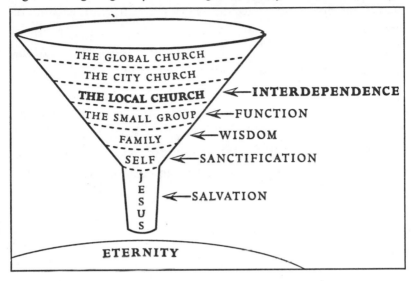

Relationship #5: The Local Church
Result: Interdependence

> It was he who gave some to be apostles, some to be prophets, some to be evangelists, and some to be pastors and teachers, to prepare God's people for works of service, so that the body of Christ may be built up until we all reach unity in the faith and in the knowledge of the Son of God and become mature, attaining to the whole measure of the fullness of Christ....From him the whole body, joined and held together by every supporting ligament, grows and builds itself up in love, as each part does its work (Eph. 4:11-13,16).

Our local churches are God's storehouses of dynamic power for learning to function in the strength of interdependence. In 1 Corinthians 12, the Bible reminds us that we are a Body with many members, which only functions when working together. By worshiping, giving, learning and growing together as a local church, our cumulative impact dramatically increases. In local churches, our unified prayer, financial strength and mutual encouragement causes us to form a Body of Christians capable of accomplishing tasks that would be impossible in small groups.

Ephesians 4:16 emphasizes the role of interdependent relationships within the local church when it talks about the Body being "joined and held together by every supporting ligament." Those supporting ligaments are the healthy relationships within the Body that cause it to grow, build itself up and work. God's plan for His people cannot be fulfilled unless we gather as a local church so the apostles, prophets, evangelists, pastors and teachers can equip us to effectively work in His kingdom.

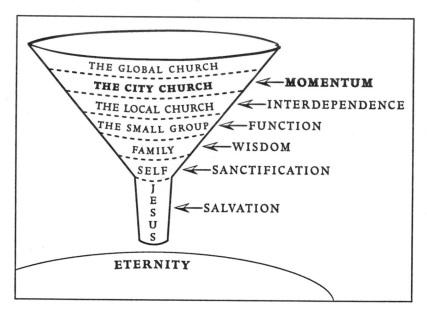

Relationship #6: The City Church
Result: Momentum

To the angel of the church in Ephesus, Smyrna, Pergamum, Thyatira, Sardis, Philadelphia and Laodicea write (see Rev. 2:1,8,12,18; 3:1,7,14).

All around the world the Holy Spirit is speaking to the Body about forming citywide coalitions of local churches to promote evangelism. These coalitions are groups of churches that strengthen one another by forming strategic alliances. The coalition of churches in Colorado Springs has three goals:

1. We pray for every person in our city by name at least once a year;
2. We communicate the gospel, in an understandable way, to every person in our city at least once a year; and
3. We want an additional 1 percent of our city's population attending church on an average weekend by the end of each year. For our city, that means an additional 3,500 people saved and discipled in our churches citywide every year.

To achieve these goals, we have several networks of churches that coordinate our citywide efforts. Individually, our churches could not have accomplished these goals; but as a group of churches, we can achieve them with relative ease. This network of relationships makes all of our jobs simpler, and causes our churches to grow through conversion growth rather than competing for transfer growth.

Just as individual Christians need to connect with others in a healthy local church in order to grow strong, so local churches can connect with other local churches to become increasingly effective. My book *Primary Purpose* (Creation House) discusses "how to make it hard to go to hell from your city." Jack Hayford and I coauthored a book on city strategies entitled, *Loving Your City into the Kingdom* (Regal Books), an excellent resource for all Christians. Bill Bright, Peter Wagner, Ed Silvoso, George Otis, Jr., George Barna and others contributed to this book. Another recommended resource for city strategies is Ed Silvoso's book *That None Should Perish* (Regal Books).

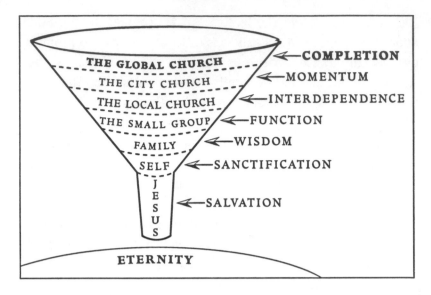

Relationship #7: The Global Church
Result: Completion

> After this I looked and there before me was a great multitude that no one could count, from every nation, tribe, people and language, standing before the throne and in front of the Lamb. They were wearing white robes and were holding palm branches in their hands (Rev. 7:9).

The final set of relationships needed to empower us for effective ministry is the network of relationships we as local churches form to enable missionary activities. These efforts require local churches to take a portion of their tithes and strategically use the money to ensure that every person living in our generation has an opportunity to hear the gospel. This level of relationships furthers our efforts to fulfill the Great Commission: "Go and make disciples of all nations, baptizing them in the name of the Father and of the Son and of the Holy Spirit, and teaching them to obey everything I have commanded you" (Matt. 28:19,20). To fulfill this task, we must work in harmony with the other members of the

Body of Christ in increasingly broader relationships. By working as members of the global church, the city church, the local church, the small group and the family, we can see Jesus' calling on our lives fulfilled.

Some will argue against various levels of these increasingly empowering relationships. However, I believe as we receive the revelation from His Spirit and the Scriptures about our purpose in His kingdom, it becomes evident that each of these sets of relationships are vital to His purpose and are dependent upon one another. Relationships are not optional for any of us as Christians. Productive, empowering relationships make ministry easy, delightful and efficient with maximum breadth of impact—they are foundational to building a life-giving church.

7

CHARACTERISTICS
THAT PROTECT

YOU [CHRIST] ARE THE MOST EXCELLENT OF MEN
AND YOUR LIPS HAVE BEEN ANOINTED WITH GRACE,
SINCE GOD HAS BLESSED YOU FOREVER. GIRD YOUR
SWORD UPON YOUR SIDE, O MIGHTY ONE; CLOTHE
YOURSELF WITH SPLENDOR AND MAJESTY. IN YOUR
MAJESTY RIDE FORTH VICTORIOUSLY IN BEHALF OF
TRUTH, HUMILITY AND RIGHTEOUSNESS; LET YOUR
RIGHT HAND DISPLAY AWESOME DEEDS.

[*Psalm 45:2-4*]

SYSTEMS THAT WOUND

Pastor Bowen watched from an upstairs window as one of the volunteers from the nursery got into her car with her three children. With snow blowing all around her, the mother carefully buckled each child safely into their old, rusted family vehicle with balding tires. After the car had a chance to warm up, it slowly crept out of the church parking lot headed for home.

Because this mom had been faithfully serving in the nursery, and obviously needed better transportation, the pastor wanted to buy the family a new set of tires, or maybe even replace their car with a newer model. Then the process started....Board members wondered if they were setting a precedent that would result in trouble with other moms in the church. Others wondered if helping this family was the wisest expenditure of church finances. Some even questioned the true faithfulness of the mother!

Pastor Bowen understood the reasoning for systems that would not allow him to randomly spend money for parishioners, but today it didn't make sense. He just wanted to help quickly and quietly, and yet now that the issue had become a major discussion, he feared the family would hear about it and be embarrassed. The board denied the money. The mom did hear about it and was embarrassed and, a few months later, quietly left the church.

This incident illustrates the need for certain characteristics within our local churches that will protect our ability to minister life. Psalm 45 prophesies about the coming Christ, and explains how Christ in His majesty will ride forth victoriously in behalf of truth, humility and righteousness, displaying awesome deeds by His right hand.

Our churches are His right hand, which is to display awesome deeds—that is why we need to be undergirded with *truth, humility* and *righteousness*. In this chapter I will discuss these three qualities which reflect the characteristics of our life-giving churches, and, in a sense, provide protective armor for them. But before we review these characteristics, it's important that we contrast and clarify the roles of the spiritual Body and the corporate structure.

SPIRITUAL MINISTRY SERVED BY CORPORATE STRUCTURE

All modern churches have two structures within them. One is the spiritual Body; the other is the corporation. Jesus Christ is the head of the spiritual Body with pastors who teach, elders who support, deacons who serve, apostles who lead, evangelists who win the lost, and overseers and bishops who bless and protect. The Bible is their guide and the Holy Spirit provides the life for this living organism, the true Church.

Membership within this spiritual Body is based on being born again. Heaven, not this world, is the home of the Church. Believers, therefore, do not have the same values as nonbelievers.

It doesn't take any money to perform the functions of the spiritual Body. Spiritual Bodies study the Scriptures and minister to others in the power of Jesus' name by the anointing of the Holy Spirit. We lead people to Christ, pray and worship—all paid for by Christ on the cross.

But if the believers who make up the spiritual Body want to use their tithes to finance missions, own a building or hire people to coordinate meetings, then the spiritual Body must form a corporation to perform these functions.

Corporations perform practical functions that do cost money. They have officers, boards and members that govern them. Corporations own assets, incur liabilities, employ personnel and set budgets. Even though the corporate side of a church is important, the corporation is the servant of the spiritual Body.

Many churches effectively use their corporations to further the ministry of the church. Too often, however, as years pass, the corporation slowly starts dominating the spiritual Body. Once this happens, the spiritual Body becomes the servant of the corporation and the purpose of believers' meetings becomes the receiving of offerings, the selling of religious products and increasing assets.

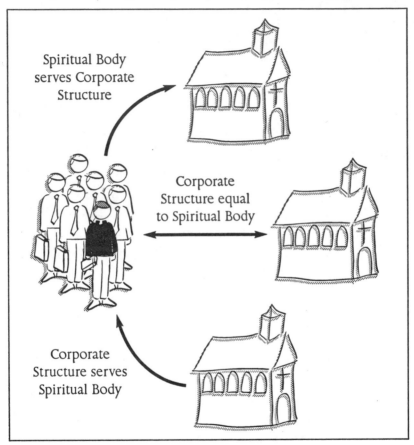

The values of most churches are usually revealed by the objectives of their leaders. If leaders focus on people coming to Christ and the stirring of faith and freedom for the Holy Spirit to minister, then the corporation is only a tool of the church. If, however, emphasis transfers to church attendance, the offering, gaining new members and/or trying to avoid offending anyone, then the church becomes no more than a resource of the corporation. Understandably, the Holy Spirit is grieved when this reversal occurs.

Recently I had lunch with a man who had just been hired by a large mainstream church as its director of evangelism. He said his primary responsibility was to bring people to membership. Because I knew that agnostics, humanists and Universalists held membership there, I realized that this church was no longer a spiritual Christian Body at all. Instead, it had become a group of members working for the corporation—to expand assets and influence by enlarging the membership.

In an attempt to prevent this process, some churches place their spiritual leaders in corporate positions, hoping to ensure that the corporation always serves the spiritual needs of the congregation. As a result, churches are sometimes poorly managed. Certainly, many spiritual leaders are competent corporate executives, but others are not. Because a person is honest, dependable and qualified as a spiritual leader, we should not assume that the person is fully equipped to buy and sell real estate, sign leases or borrow money. Many are not.

Therefore, various attempts have been made to develop systems that protect the spiritual Body while utilizing the strength of the corporation. Thus, we now have a combination of four major church governance systems: (1) strong pastoral leadership, (2) board, eldership or presbyter authority, (3) congregational control or (4) outside denominational oversight. Every church is governed by one or some combination of these systems.

Much of the confusion within the church is caused by tension over money, struggles over the control of assets and influence over others. Therefore, life-giving churches must wisely distinguish between the legal corporation and the spiritual Body. By clearly defining these roles, the resulting order and peace will allow members to stay in the tree of life and perform the ministries of the spiritual Body. This distinction is clearly articulated in chapter 14, "Bylaws."

The following characteristics are necessary for both the corporate structure and the spiritual Body of the church. When truth, humility and righteousness are in operation, the freedom and innocence of the church are protected. With the discussions of each characteristic, I have given tips for implementing these characteristics into the lives of the leadership and the church.

Truth

> When Jesus spoke again to the people, he said, "I am the light of the world. Whoever follows me will never walk in darkness, but will have the light of life" (John 8:12).

1. Be honorable and honest.

Paul says in Ephesians 4:1 and 2, "I urge you to live a life worthy of the calling you have received. Be completely humble and gentle; be patient, bearing with one another in love." Living a life worthy of the calling includes obeying the commandments: Don't lie and steal. Don't be deceitful. Demonstrate integrity through actions rather than honorable words.

As leaders, we communicate commitment to the church and community when we *buy* a home rather than *rent*. This says we're here to stay; we're not just passing through. We are wise to drive a moderately priced car rather than one that communicates extravagance or unnecessary spending. And we demonstrate prudence when we refuse to dress like a television personality, especially since we aren't one. Even when we do appear on television, it's best to dress reasonably. And as for the flattering words that may come our way, we must not believe them—they're exaggerations. Scripture warns us against thinking more highly of ourselves than we ought (see Rom. 12:3). We are to humbly serve the Body by actually being who God wants us to be, and doing what He wants us to do. We are to reflect Him, not the world.

2. Fast and pray.

Regularly scheduled times of constructive, proactive, private prayer and fasting are a powerful way to rest, recharge your spirit and clarify God's plan and power in your heart. While praying and fasting, don't get introspective and depressed, instead let the truth of the Word and the power of His blood cleanse you so you can effectively serve in His kingdom for many years.

The strength of prayer and fasting combined with regular Bible reading and prayer will help establish priorities. As a result, you'll get more done. A godly pace established by accurate priorities keeps us from ever having to be deceitful or fake, and it protects us against burnout.

3. No secrets.

I believe *there is no such thing as a secret*, which helps me stay clean. When opportunities are presented that require secrecy, I don't do them. That's the way we keep our consciences clean and, as a result, the light of truth is our friend, not our enemy.

4. Be purpose driven.

Successful leaders know why they do what they do. The apostle Paul maintained his ministry purposes in the midst of complex church situations. Paul was motivated by the love of Christ and the terror of hell, and that revelation propelled his ministry (see 2 Cor. 5:11,14).

Keeping a clear perspective about why we're doing what we're doing is vital. Many people who truly love God have become disillusioned with church because we often fail to articulate why we meet together. Understanding and pursuing clear-cut objectives without unnecessary clutter has great public appeal.

5. Financial integrity is a close friend.

Many people love giving to God but resent the schemes some churches use to raise money. When believers see honesty, integrity and genuine spiritual values reflected in the business of the church and the lifestyles of their church leaders, they are much more willing to give generously. Every year we publish our cash-flow statement and send it to all contributors with their contribution statements. Why not?! We have nothing to hide.

6. Honor the tithe and don't get greedy.
Jesus said, "Come to me, all you who are weary and burdened, and I will give you *rest.* Take my yoke upon you and learn from me, for I am gentle and humble in heart, and you will find rest for your souls. For my yoke is *easy* and my burden is *light*" (Matt. 11:28-30, italics added). Did He say easy and light?

———

IT'S OUR RESPONSIBILITY TO MANAGE THE
DISTRIBUTION OF THE TITHE IN A GODLY WAY.
IT'S NOT OUR RESPONSIBILITY TO GET
PEOPLE TO GIVE MORE.

———

In 2 Corinthians 11:9, the apostle Paul reveals that he refused payment for ministry because he didn't want ministry expenses to be a burden for believers. Did he say he didn't want ministry to be a burden?

Obviously the Bible teaches powerful principles about sowing and reaping, and every Christian must participate in sowing seed into God's storehouse in order to receive the full blessings God wants to give.

The giving of tithes and offerings is worship to God. If any one of us ever tampers with or defiles worship, God will respond. For that reason, I am very cautious. In order to avoid the pressure to become manipulative with offerings, we set our budgets based on past history rather than upward projections. And as a result, even though we have grown more than 10 percent every year for 13 consecutive years, the financial support of the church has never been a burden to the believers.

It's our responsibility to manage the distribution of the tithe in a godly way. It's not our responsibility to get people to give more.

7. Don't drain baby churches dry.

Some church plants unnecessarily struggle because all of the financial resources are absorbed with the pastoral salary and/or a building. I recommend using a percentage system in the beginning. We used a scale such as the following:

35%	Pastor and/or staff
10%	Missions
10%	Youth
10%	Outreach (to promote the gospel in our city)
35%	Facilities (building, utilities, etc.)

This scale was excellent in the early stages to infuse life into our birthing baby church.

8. Whatever you build it on, you'll have to maintain it on.

If you build the church on Sunday School, you will have to maintain it with Sunday School. If you build the church with great guest speakers, you will have to maintain it with great guest speakers. If it's powerful preaching, you'll have to maintain it on that. If you build on prophecy, you're in trouble if the Holy Spirit doesn't want to give a prophecy. Let all these ministries be tools, but build the church on worship and the Word of God so you can maintain steady growth. Remember, "flesh gives birth to flesh, but the Spirit gives birth to spirit" (John 3:6).

Humility

Humility and the fear of the Lord bring wealth and honor and life (Prov. 22:4).

The one characteristic God positively responds to from Genesis through Revelation is humility. Humility does not mean weakness or powerlessness, but instead indicates clear understanding of authority, spiritual power and holiness. Thus, the humble are meek, modest and submissive.

These attitudes always activate supernatural favor. Thus, the Bible promises that as we understand how to relate to others with humility rather than arrogance, it opens the door for our ministries to enjoy wealth, honor and life (Prov. 22:4).

The following are seven practices that require humility and provide protection for our churches:

1. Foster freedom with simple structures.
We must set people free, both spiritually and within the structure of the church. To offer freedom in Christ and, at the same time, force people to navigate through complex ministry structures is counterproductive. They won't do it.

The gospel message is simple enough to be grasped by all, and we certainly should not cloud participation in the church with structures that are excessively bureaucratic.

2. Promote membership in Christ's Body.
Jesus is the Head of the Church, and people are ultimately responsible to Him. Life-giving churches emphasize the goodness of knowing Him, not necessarily the church. Because of this fact, we at New Life emphasize membership in the Body of Christ and a commitment to Him above membership in our specific church and commitment to us. We are at best the instrument God will use to save, heal or restore people, but God actually does the work.

3. Give others the freedom to choose.
Because the Lord gives people the freedom to make decisions and then receive the benefits or the consequences, we stay in the tree of life with greater ease when we respect their decisions.

The primary responsibility of the pastor and other staff leaders is to equip believers for ministry, to encourage good choices through Bible teaching and counsel, to pray, and to lovingly correct and administer the day-to-day affairs of the church. These roles do not include personal control or manipulation of people's lives. This freedom allows people to feel respected, responsible and accepted.

Everyone needs a pastor, Pastor! Every pastor should have another pastor that he or she looks to for wisdom, counsel and spiritual covering. My pastors are Roy and Larry Stockstill of Bethany World Prayer Center in Baker, Louisiana. Every year one of them visits New Life and is introduced as my pastor. Their covering provides stability, consistency and security for both the congregation and me.

4. Develop and maintain the heart of a servant.
Make sure a servant's attitude saturates the entire church Body. People don't owe the leadership anything. On the contrary, leaders owe service to everyone the Lord sends across their path. Treat all people as though they were gifts from God. Serve people in such a way that God can trust you; then He will add more to you.

The balance to this is the reality that sometimes people will take advantage of you, drain your energy and steal your time. Even these people can be dealt with from a servant's attitude, but this doesn't mean you're always soft and fluffy. To serve people, it is often necessary to be firm and direct, in love.

5. Promote Jesus, not the church.
Churches often waste huge amounts of money advertising themselves. I know it's hard to believe, but people don't care as much about you or your church as you think; they do care about God. So by promoting what He does, the Holy Spirit may choose to promote you. And when He does, it will be because you are His representative, not your own.

6. Laugh more and enjoy people.

Laughing at things that, if taken seriously, could become major issues, makes ministry much more fun. Just laugh and go on. When God is in control, circumstances can't move out of His hand and become crises. Trust God. Enjoy the variety of people. Never put them down or become critical. Avoid classifying groups of people. Remember that they are individuals, not groups. Every person is the way he or she is for a reason. Should you be tempted to err in relationships, always err on the side of grace.

7. Learn.

In order to be increasingly effective for many years, we have to be humble enough to identify those who know certain areas of ministry better than we do and learn from them. Read their books, attend their conferences and study their churches. My practice is to learn from others and wait six months to see what ideas still impact me—then apply them. The fresh input keeps us growing, while the six-month waiting period prevents us from swinging from trend to trend too quickly. We don't want to be movement-oriented churches; we want to be steady, increasingly effective churches.

Another set of teachers that helps us improve our influence on others is our critics. In our office, we refer to our critics as our Tuesday mail: We upset them on Sunday, they write on Monday, and we read on Tuesday. These people give us helpful information if we'll look past their anger and determine whether or not they have a point. I think Tuesday mail can sometimes be our best friend. My practice is to read all mail that is signed. If it is anonymous, I don't read it. For me to hear them, they must believe it enough to identify themselves.

Righteousness

"For I tell you that unless your righteousness surpasses that of the Pharisees and the teachers of the law, you will certainly not enter the kingdom of heaven" (Matt. 5:20).

Every believer enjoys the way the Word of God and the Holy Spirit breathe Jesus' righteousness into our lives. That righteousness, which is freely given to us by God, is not only reflected in our personal lifestyles but also in the ministries we are able to influence. Life-giving churches have additional strength because of the righteousness reflected in their foundational philosophies. The following are six of those ideas:

1. Establish efficient church governments.

As I mentioned previously, godly people often become disillusioned with the carnality of church politics and business meetings. Therefore, we encourage:

- Strong pastoral leadership in the day-to-day operations of the church;
- Board-of-trustee control in major financial decisions;
- Full congregational rule in the selection of a new senior pastor; and
- Outside eldership (overseers) jurisdiction when disciplining the senior pastor.

This system clearly separates the various roles within the Body, and allows us to benefit from the most positive elements of the four primary types of church government. With the peace this balance brings, believers are free to grow without the burden of an excessive church government. The church was designed to be a place of liberty, healthy growth and development, not a burden. Relax and keep it simple.

2. Structure and plan for the church to last longer than you do.

Remember, we are working in God's kingdom, not our own. If Jesus doesn't return soon, others will inherit the churches we serve. To ensure that our work will continue long after we die or retire, we must structure our churches so others can minister through them for generations to come.

Because the church belongs to Jesus and not to a pastor or a particular group of people, it should be structured to provide ministry through a variety of people. The Bylaws explained in chapter 14 were written with that thinking in mind.

3. Conservatively address the senior pastor's salary.

It seems as though we have two streams of thought. One group underpays pastors, and their families suffer as a result. The other group pays the senior pastor so well that his lifestyle seems contradictory to the mission of the church.

To balance those extremes, I recommend that pastors have the ability to set their own salaries with certain provisions and restrictions. That way the pastor is rewarded for successfully serving a church, and his other associates are adequately paid as well. Chapter 14 explains the details of this approach.

4. Focus on the gospel.

Extremely positive, healing messages should be taught in conjunction with regular personal power ministry. Teach life, not law. Display greater wisdom than Adam and Eve. Reject the temptation to feed your followers from the tree of knowledge of good and evil, but instead let them grow from the tree of life. Stick with living water, the bread of life and His fruit in their lives.

If you start teaching the knowledge of good and evil, your people will be poisoned and die. If you teach life, they will live and prosper and grow. Remember as you teach that the issues are life and death, not good and evil. No matter what your subject is, always edify.

5. Fight the devil; serve people.

Don't fight with city hall, the neighbors, other Christian groups or the atheists. Serve them. Obey the law. Fight only the devil and serve people. "For our struggle is not against flesh and blood, but against the rulers, against the authorities, against the powers of this dark world and against the spiritual forces of evil in the heavenly realms" (Eph. 6:12). Do battle in your prayer closet and serve in public.

6. Encourage free-market ministry.

Free-market ministries always produce creative and innovative ministry methods. Anywhere in the world where the government allows a free-market economy, people produce goods and services that make prosperity possible. In contrast, where central-command economies are dictated from a central office, the result is always poor quality, poor service and outdated products—unhappy people.

Our local churches have some of the same characteristics. When we allow the Holy Spirit to work within people to create effective ministries, we have an abundant supply. If, on the other hand, we want to monitor every ministry from our central office, then the ministries of the church will eventually lack creativity and fail to adequately meet the needs of the congregation.

So life-giving churches should give people systems to use for their ministries. Our responsibility is to enable people to birth ministry; it is not our responsibility to make their ministries work. If they do work, praise God.

This free-market ministry style is used to one degree or another through every super-megachurch in the world. Cell systems allow people to creatively minister to others without having to initiate a program within the church. Rather than having the church leadership team create a ministry and enlist people to participate in it, cell churches allow the needs of people to create the ministries.

As we teach people to spot needs and fill them as servants, effective ministries are constantly birthing within our churches. Make sure all ministry programs center on taking care of people, not people taking care of the programs.

Together these three characteristics, truth, humility and righteousness, shield the flow of life within a church. And each of these characteristics contributes to longevity in ministry. But before we close this section on the philosophies of life-giving churches, we need to address the sensitive subject of etiquette.

What do we do when people want to leave our churches? What should we do when we want to leave? How should we treat an associate who wants to quit? All of these questions and more need to be answered if our hearts are to stay clean throughout years of ministry.

Offensive behavior among coworkers in the Body often disappoints people and hardens their hearts, causing them to make horrible mistakes. With common courtesy, though, mistakes can be avoided so, in the midst of difficult decisions, an atmosphere of harmony and life can prevail.

8

ETIQUETTE THAT SUSTAINS

DO NOTHING OUT OF SELFISH AMBITION OR VAIN
CONCEIT, BUT IN HUMILITY CONSIDER OTHERS
BETTER THAN YOURSELVES. EACH OF YOU SHOULD
LOOK NOT ONLY TO YOUR OWN INTERESTS,
BUT ALSO TO THE INTERESTS OF OTHERS.

[*Philippians 2:3,4*]

BAD ΠΑΠΠERS ΠOCK OUR
ΠΙΠΙSTRIES AΠD ΠARK OUR FUTURE

Several years ago, Bruce Jefferson, the youth pastor at Mountain
View Assembly, received what he believed to be a call from the
Lord to serve as a senior pastor. He began discussing his plans
with several church members who offered support, and before
long, Bruce was assured that the time had come for him to plant
a church. He hadn't spoken to his senior pastor about the matter
until the day he met in the pastor's study to announce his departure. The senior pastor was surprised but accepted the decision.

Bruce started a new church with his supporters from
Mountain View. Now, years later, Bruce has moved to a different
town to serve in another church, and the small church he birthed
struggles to survive. Mountain View has never regained the
momentum it lost from the departure of Bruce and his followers.
Bruce's lack of understanding about etiquette resulted in an
improper response to God's call upon his life and diminished his
reputation. Security in ministry is no longer an option for Bruce
because he didn't practice a code of behavior that enables
healthy long-term relationships.

My major fear in writing this chapter on etiquette is that I
don't want to sound like the Miss Manners of the church world.
God help me! But at the same time, we've all seen people who
have effectively ministered the life of God to others and yet were
unable to sustain their ministries because they didn't understand
the social graces of the church world. The kingdom of God suf-
fers when a believer violates decorum within the Body.

Long-term relationships cannot survive without manners.
Families that enjoy harmony do so because of a code of behavior
in the home. Public gatherings cannot be successful unless people have courtesy toward one another. Respecting others and

knowing how to make people feel comfortable is what causes society to work smoothly. That is why we in the church world need a protocol as much as any other group.

This chapter will briefly review two sets of etiquette for Christian leaders. The first set is for the senior pastor, the second for associates. As with any other relationship, both parties must use wisdom and take responsibility for their own attitudes and actions.

PROTOCOL FOR THE SENIOR PASTOR

Inter-Pastoral Friendships

When arriving in a new city, I recommend locating the ministers' gatherings and attending them regularly for at least the first year you are in town. If the pastors of the large churches attend those meetings, make a point to meet them. If they don't, call and make an appointment to meet personally with them. These pastors are the gatekeepers of the city, and their views will help you quickly orient to the community. Your presence at the meetings will help to establish a solid set of friendships that will strengthen your entire tenure in the city. After one year, go to the pastors' meetings only when you want to.

After your first year in town, you are in a position to welcome new pastors into your city. I try to get the phone numbers of pastors who will be moving to Colorado Springs so I can call to welcome them before they arrive. I offer to answer any questions they might have and assure them that they will enjoy the spiritual climate and pastoral relationships within our city. These phone calls dispel a great deal of fear and apprehension between the pastors and their new assignments, and give them a friendly point of reference once they get here.

Another courtesy that promotes inter-pastoral friendships is offering financial assistance to expanding churches. New Life doesn't generally send financial assistance to struggling churches, simply because it's important that free-market dynamics determine whether or not churches survive. But if a pastor's family is suffering because of a downward spiral in the church, we will sometimes send money to the pastor so his family can experience some relief.

If a neighboring church is doing any kind of construction to upgrade its facilities, we send some money to help. Or, if a church is celebrating an anniversary or a grand opening, we always send flowers and a card. Once a few churches start displaying this kind of support for one another, it becomes the culture of your city, which facilitates longevity in pastoral positions and the life of God flowing through churches...because of good manners.

Resigning

I believe senior pastors need to find their life call and stay in the same church and community as long as possible. I also believe it takes four years to meet someone, which means it also takes four years to meet a church and, in fact, it takes four years to begin substantive ministry within a church.

The standard I use to determine longevity in a church is whether or not it is growing. After the first four years of orientation, the church should begin growing steadily by at least 10 percent a year. If it does, stay. If it doesn't, try to correct the problem within the next year. If the church still won't grow, move on. Don't blame anyone or anything, just humble yourself and learn from the experience, then try again in another city.

The exceptions to this four-year standard are obvious: a declining population in the region, a limited population base or some other influence totally outside of your control. But in most situations, this standard works.

That being said, I understand that situations do arise when it is the genuine leading of God and/or a practical necessity to resign from a church. In those instances, always talk with the church leadership first, announce your departure to the congregation, and leave fully supporting the church. Nothing negative, critical, judgmental or offensive should be said in this process. And if negative attitudes have taken root in your heart, don't leave because of them. Hurt or bitterness will prevent you from growing in Christlikeness and can be the springboard for a long season of barrenness. Senior pastors should only leave when their hearts are clean.

STRUCTURES DON'T RESTORE

PEOPLE TO GODLY LEADERSHIP,

FRIENDS DO.

If you are moving because of the weather, don't tell the congregation that God is calling you somewhere else; tell them you're moving because of the weather. If you were fired, don't say you received a better opportunity; tell people the church leadership felt the position was not suited for you, and that you agree. If you are tired, just say it.

Graciously, wisely, and with discretion tell the truth. Don't cloak your departure in religious deception. And, don't be unkind. Instead, be gracious and truthful so every possible positive relationship can be sustained.

Hiring and Firing Staff Members

I believe senior pastors should work for the church, and staff members should work for the senior pastor. To have an effective team, senior pastors must be able to build and trim their own staff. I hire people who have both skill and personality. I enjoy ministering with people I like, therefore, I hire my friends. I hire people toward whom I have a divine flow.

Ten people at New Life report directly to me, and they are a delight for me to work with. I encourage each of them to hire people they enjoy, so the atmosphere in the office is pleasant, and we can work hard together. The friendships make the work relationships fun.

My responsibility to my friends is to assist them in fulfilling God's best plan for their lives. When their positions do not appear to be suitable, I wait six months to make sure that my assessment is correct. If it is, I talk and work with them to help find the best possible alternative. In some instances we try a different position within the church; in other cases, that is not possible.

I attempt to be flexible in this process so, together, we can find the role for that person which will be most productive for God's kingdom. Sometimes while we're searching, people continue in their positions at the church; other times, we let them go so they will have more time to locate a new position. Either way I maintain close communication and finance them beyond reason to assist in their transition.

Oh, one last note: no resignations or dismissals on Mondays.

Restoration of the Fallen

Structures don't restore people to godly leadership, friends do. I've never known of anyone who has fallen into sin and been successfully restored by the formal church structure. Nor have I ever seen a formal church structure wisely deal with sin, enabling ministry to continue without interruption. I do, however, know of many instances where a leader has fallen and that leader's friends have helped to heal and restore the person, while the church itself didn't skip a beat.

The greatest test of character is our response to someone else's sin. If our responses are from the tree of the knowledge of good and evil, which emphasizes punishment instead of restoration, judgment instead of redemption or justice instead of mercy, then our responses might sow seeds that will ultimately destroy our own lives. But if our responses are out of the tree of life, we will not only protect our own hearts from subtle deception, but will give the one who is in trouble maximum opportunity to find liberating life.

DON'T PUNISH PEOPLE WHO REPENT;

HEAL THEM.

In my view, healthy relationships best contain the temptation to unknowingly develop sinful attitudes while dealing with someone else's sin. But simple corporate roles seldom withstand the pressure and collapse into arrogance or religious high-mindedness. Friends cry with friends over failure and get people healed; supervisors without strong relationships seldom do.

So how do we restore the fallen? First, sin only needs to be repented of as far as it has actually gone. Forgiveness doesn't have to be asked for from people who don't know that the sin ever occurred. So if a brother or sister falls, get him or her with trusted friends and have the person repent to everyone who has been violated. If the person repents, establish a simple but purposeful restoration plan and have friends assist and monitor the recovery.

Don't punish people who repent; heal them. I don't believe private sin requires public rebuke or removal from office if repentance is taking place. However, when no evidence of true repentance exists, then discipline is in order.

In every step of restoration, be sure to ask: *What do we hope to accomplish from the action we are considering?* And, *Will this produce positive results for the kingdom of God?* When repentance is present, there is a time when love should cover sin.

In these situations, mercy prevails over justice (see Jas. 2:13). But if repentance is not evident, then and only then should justice and judgment prevail.

Visiting Speakers

Before inviting guest speakers to our church, we make sure the following five questions have been answered:

1. *Can we pay them well?* When speakers accept our invitation, leaving their normal routines, families and all other duties to be with us, we recognize that the opportunity costs began when they started packing for the trip and those costs won't end until they are settled back into their routines at home. So we cover all of their expenses, except phone calls and personal purchases, and reward their families for their time away from home. When we invite pastors to speak in one of our Sunday services, we understand that they must be away from their church on Sunday—a major opportunity cost that deserves to be rewarded.

2. *Can we host them well?* Different people like to be hosted differently. I like to be picked up at the airport and driven to my hotel room. Or, if I must travel a long distance from the airport, I prefer to rent a car with a good map. But I don't like staying in people's homes unless absolutely necessary. Why? Because they want to host me when I need to rest or work. I don't mind, though, meeting with as many people as possible who are associated with the reason for my visit.

3. *Can we communicate with them well?* When I travel, I want to know why I'm there, how many people I'm going to be speaking to, the appropriate dress for the event and any protocol issues that might be relevant. If communication is not clear, then I'll choose the topic I

teach on, which might not fulfill my host's expectations. Therefore, clear written communication in advance is very important.

4. *Can we introduce them well?* The purpose of an introduction is to prevent speakers from having to spend the first 15 minutes of their talk connecting with the crowd. If the introduction is warm and includes meaningful information, it will communicate the speaker's right to be heard. Reading from a biography is acceptable, but reading it for the first time in front of the crowd is not.

5. *Will inviting this speaker hurt any of the nearby churches that have previously hosted this person?* Sometimes we would like to have a certain speaker but, because that person has often been with another local church, we might appear to be doing something unethical if we were to ask that person to speak at our church.

Responding to Those Who Are Leaving

One of the most difficult situations a senior pastor ever faces is the departure of a valued staff member or family from the church. I believe in dialoguing with people when they are considering a major transition. With some, the discussions should occur as friends. With others, it should occur as a pastor talking with an associate or parishioner. Unfortunately, with some staff members, the dialogue is purely a discussion between an employer and an employee. Each of these roles has its own standards of etiquette and rules of conduct.

Most tension, however, develops when the culture of the church does not allow easy entrance and comfortable exit. My experience has been that if people have the freedom to go in good graces, they will sense a greater freedom to choose to stay. I encourage full discussion when thoughts of leaving first develop, unless of course the departing staff member or parishioner chooses not to communicate and has already made a decision to go. In those instances, the pastor should not dialogue extensively with the person, but cordially accept the decision. Don't be cold, just graciously accept it.

The only exception to this standard is when, for valid reasons, you know the decision is wrong. Then, you can protest, but not as a pastor or as an employer, only as a friend. Friends can passionately discuss delicate issues such as this; however, it violates every sense of dignity, courtesy and good taste to have a pastor or employer resist the departure of a staff member or parishioner.

So how do we treat those who have gone? With decorum: kind words, gracious conversation and cordiality. Never should the senior pastor become harsh, judgmental or condemning. Instead the senior pastor should treat those who have gone with respect and affection.

But what about rejection? I feel rejected when people just disappear or announce their decision to depart. I do, however, understand that those things will happen for good reasons, and I respect that. But it is easier if I, or someone else on the staff, is part of the process and was a part of the conclusion. Then, no matter how we feel about the decision, at least we can understand it.

PROTOCOL FOR ASSOCIATE PASTORS

Your First Day on the Job
Every church has a secret code of conduct that everyone on staff knows about, except you, the new associate.

I'll never forget my first day of work at Bethany World Prayer Center, the megachurch of Baton Rouge, Louisiana. I arrived early as the new associate pastor: clean shoes, crisp shirt and sharp suit. I was ready to minister. But it didn't happen. Instead, Brother Roy, the senior pastor, began educating me in the culture of Bethany by gently saying with a grin, "Brother Ted, go home and get some work clothes on; we'll be picking up sticks today." I understood perfectly. I was in for a series of lessons about social graces that were going to have to be caught through observation, not taught with words. It took two years.

The first day for every associate pastor lasts about two years. During this time, three relationships have to be developed. The first is your relationship with the senior pastor. Learn his personality, his moods, his likes and dislikes. Don't judge him, just serve him. Make him glad you are there.

The second significant relationship to cultivate is with other associates. They know all of the unspoken rules, so watch them closely. They understand how and when to dress; when to be visible and when to disappear; and how to get the job done. But they won't know what to think of you until you've been there a while, so stay steady. Have a servant's heart, and yet serve with confidence. Don't be arrogant, but don't be a puppy. Just stay humble.

As these first two relationships are developing, the door will open for a significant relationship with the congregation itself. As the pastor gets to know you and the other associates begin to respect you, you will enter into effective ministry within the congregation. It will feel great, but remember the process takes about two years.

These first two years will include lessons on personality styles, power, wisdom and patience. Building for a successful future is tied closely with your ability to patiently stay innocent as you learn. If you give the impression that you are impatient, disloyal, high-minded or just waiting for a better offer, people will only superficially connect with you. Conversely, if you make a decision to relate with people as if you're going to stay for the rest of your life, you might actually receive that option.

As you work through your first two years, develop a healthy pattern of praying and fasting, daily Bible reading, and serving with confidence and humility. Don't brag or even talk much about your spiritual discipline, just do it. Make the senior pastor's job easier, and understand that both you and the senior pastor will have different expectations as time passes. Don't let your original expectations limit you, instead stay flexible so your strengths can find your most productive role within the church.

Multiple Roles in Relationships

If your goal is to develop a positive and healthy relationship with the pastor, you must understand the multiple roles he will have in your life: associate in ministry, friend, intercessor, defender, confidant, employer, traveling companion and basketball buddy—all at the same time. These different roles can become very confusing.

To successfully serve as an associate pastor, you will have to learn these various roles. Early in the day, the senior pastor may be your friend. When he calls you that evening, he is your boss. The next morning when you see him in church, he's your spiritual leader. But on Monday when you play basketball with him, he's an old man with a bad back.

Occasionally when meeting with my staff, decorum requires that I distinguish our roles. I'll openly say that this conversation is friend to friend, or church business, or whatever. Clarifying the roles can help, but most associates usually know which role I'm in at the time.

But I Have a Call on My Life Too!

For churches to grow, many more people must be called to be associates than senior pastors. New Life Church has many pastors, but only one senior pastor. Because of my style, we function as a team; however, the buck stops with me.

Every pastor on our staff has a strong sense of purpose, and I pray that their purpose will be fulfilled at New Life. Out of love and respect for them, I do everything I can to see that their dreams are fulfilled and that the desires within their hearts are satisfied. Therefore, the vast majority of our pastors have served in various roles within our church. Communication and flexibility allow the transitions to protect everyone's dignity as the years pass and as our ministries grow.

I deeply love and appreciate every day of working with the pastoral team God has placed at New Life. Yet I understand that as they go through the various stages of life, their hearts can become restless and at times they sense the call of God to go pastor a church themselves. Even though I hate it, my responsibility as their friend and pastor is to assist them in doing what's right for themselves and the kingdom of God.

Can I Work at Another Church in Town?

Yes, but certain rules apply. For example, it is improper for any leader to take a position in another church within the same city unless the senior pastor has made the arrangements to do so. When the associate has independently arranged the move to a nearby church, a major violation of protocol and a betrayal of the Kingdom occurs. It feels too much like a divorce. It betrays a sacred trust.

The sacred trust is also violated when an associate takes a senior pastor's position in a nearby church without the senior pastor's initiative. A pastor moving to a neighboring church should never confuse relationships established in another local church. Subjecting believers to awkward situations such as these is unwise and unproductive. It's poor judgment, and causes believers to feel like children whose parents are divorcing. Don't do it.

I Think God Is Calling Me to Plant a Church

A worse violation of common courtesy occurs when an associate leaves to plant a church nearby. This is the ultimate violation of any sense of social grace and is an offense to God.

Associates who resign or are dismissed should not serve in a church or plant a church within a one-hour drive of their previous church. *The Haggard one-hour rule.*

But what if the senior pastor is wrong? Gene Edward's book

The Tale of Three Kings, beautifully addresses this situation. I suggest reading it if you have a moral dilemma regarding the senior pastor.

How do I quit so I can move on? If you want to consider becoming a senior pastor or taking another position outside of the church which would require a resignation, talk with your pastor about it. If open communication is established with the pastor, and the change is the right thing to do, resigning should not be uncomfortable. It is important to leave the church in good standing. The pastor can tell you if the timing is good, or if he would rather you stay for an additional few months. A request to stay more than a year would be excessive, however, I have found that when I have asked an associate to stay a few months to help the church through a particular season, the delay has generally benefited both of us.

Longevity in Ministry

Later in this book we discuss pay schedules and structures that encourage longevity in ministry. Staying in one location for an extended period of time is not only personally beneficial to growing our ministries, but is also beneficial for the kingdom of God.

Unless you know, without any doubt, that you are supposed to serve as a senior pastor, ask God to place you in a church with a strong calling, and faithfully serve there. As the years pass, the church will develop and strengthen, and you'll find that staying with the same people year after year in a growing church is deeply satisfying.

No matter where you serve, you will be successful if you remain in the tree of life, flowing in innocence and the anointing. You will then be able to maintain an environment where the gifts and fruit of the Holy Spirit provide life-giving nourishment for others and a reputation that reflects Kingdom values and Kingdom etiquette.

Section III

Ministries of a Life-Giving Church

9. Multiplication of Life: Missions

10. Impartation of Life: Worship
    By *Ross Parsley*

11. Integration of Life: Free Market Cells
    With *Russ Walker*

12. Demonstration of Life: Elders
    With *Lance Coles*

Even though life-giving churches have a variety of ministries, I have selected four from New Life Church that reflect the philosophy of life-giving ministry. These four—Missions, Worship, Free Market Cells and Elders—are just examples of light, innocent, life-giving ideals to study and apply.

As you read this section, pay close attention to not only the practices described but also the philosophy behind them. Then apply that philosophy to any ministry to make it increasingly life-giving.

9

MULTIPLICATION OF LIFE: MISSIONS

ASK THE LORD OF THE HARVEST,
THEREFORE, TO SEND OUT WORKERS
INTO HIS HARVEST FIELD.

[*Matthew 9:38*]

One Life to Give

The soldiers forced the family to stand on the beach for more than an hour without telling them why they were there or what they were going to do. The family members only knew that Mom had been summoned to school earlier that day for questioning about her faith. She had been accused of telling her children about God—accusations that were true. A month earlier during their evening meal the mother of these seven children had told them about the Savior and His great love for them.

Everyone in the family knew the school had heard about their discussion from one of the youngest children, but no one dared say anything about it. As they stood on the beach glancing nervously at one another and, at times, looking away in anguish, fear began to mount.

The silence was suddenly interrupted by the rumble of converging military trucks. After coming to a dusty halt on the beach, the officers sternly exited their vehicles and approached the family, visually inspecting each family member, especially the parents. A group of young soldiers began to unload a barrel from the back of a truck and rolled it toward the water. The barrel was open on one end.

For no apparent reason, the guards lifted their rifles toward the family, forcing them to stand in a row. Then the dreaded command came, ordering the mother to step forward. She handed the youngest, who had been tightly clinging to her, to her husband. Her body quaked with fear as she began slowly walking toward the guards. Father watched in terror. And the youngest, knowing that everything was very wrong, started to cry. With several rifles pointed in her direction, the officers ordered this godly woman into the barrel where her frail body was forced into a fetal position.

Mother was affectionately studying her family when her head disappeared into the barrel. The children screamed. Daddy shouted something, but one of the guards threatened him, and he stopped. Then a guard approached the oldest boy, 17-year-old Palucha, pointing a pistol at his head and ordering him to step forward. Palucha reluctantly obeyed. The guard handed Palucha the lid to the barrel with a hammer and nails, and commanded him to seal his own mother in the barrel.

Palucha refused at first, but caught his mother's eyes and listened as she softly beckoned him to obey the soldiers. She said she understood and wanted him to obey, explaining that they would see each other in another world. Palucha heaved in sorrow as he placed the lid on the barrel and nailed it shut.

The soldiers forced the family to watch as they rolled the barrel into the sea. Older family members held the littlest ones in their arms to keep them from running after their mother. Then, with the sudden crack of rifle shots, the guards started shooting at the barrel.

This family has never known whether their mother died from gunshot wounds or drowning. There were never any sounds from the sinking barrel. They only knew that the same fate awaited anyone in their communist state who expressed a belief in the living God.

Afterward, the guards turned to the family and said, "There is no God. He didn't help her, and He won't help you." The trucks drove off, leaving the grieving family standing alone on the beach while their dead mother sank to the bottom of the sea in her coffin, a crude barrel. They were alone; their mother was a martyr.

FULFILLING THE PRAYERS
OF THE MARTYRS

Since the fall of Communism in Europe, no one has been able to confirm this story, but when I heard it and others like it in college, my worldview changed dramatically. As a 20-year-old college student, I would walk around the campus in the evenings, asking God to use me to serve the suffering Church. I knew the martyrs had asked God to protect their families and save their countries. As I considered their bravery and sacrifice, I realized there could be no greater honor in this life than to be used by God to answer some of the prayers that were prayed in those barrels.

Just before graduation from college, I received a phone call from World Missions for Jesus, a West German missions organization, saying that they were looking for someone to help establish a stronger North American office. When I heard that World Missions served the suffering Church in atheistic countries, I agreed to meet with them.

I accepted the position with World Missions for Jesus, and the perspective I learned there and in my subsequent position at Bethany World Prayer Center convinced me that every church should take advantage of every opportunity to impact the world for Christ. Life-giving churches don't exist for themselves, but for those who don't know life Himself, Christ. God has spoken that same message to lots of people. That's why many life-giving churches are missions churches.

OTHERS, THE FOCUS OF THE CHURCH

The Bible teaches that all believers should tithe to the storehouse, which I believe is the local church. I also believe local churches should tithe to missions. At New Life, we budget at least 10 percent for missions. But because of the way God always blesses our church, we usually find ourselves giving more than 20 percent of our total income to missions. Our church gave more than $1 million to missions last year to help answer some prayers that were prayed in the barrels.

When Jesus was exhorting His disciples just before His ascension, He said, "But you will receive power when the Holy Spirit comes on you; and you will be my witnesses in Jerusalem, and in all Judea and Samaria, and to the ends of the earth" (Acts 1:8). His exhortation applies to every one of us.

In chapter 5 we discussed how this verse prepared the disciples to receive the power of the Holy Spirit. But the power of the Holy Spirit was not given to enable the Early Church to have better church services; it was given to provide the Church with the power to reach unbelievers. Outreach starts in our "Jerusalems," our hometowns, then our "Judeas," the state or nation surrounding our hometowns. "Samaria" is a neighboring state, in this case a despised state to the north of Judea. And "to the ends of the earth" exhorts us to ensure that every people group is reached!

THE REASON GOD GIVES US HIS LIFE
IS TO IMPACT OUR WORLD.

The reason God gives us His life is to impact our world.

New Life has a very specific strategy for staying outreach oriented. We have flags hanging in the living room, our main auditorium, from every nation on earth. We also fly the flags of Native American nations, the United Nations, the Presidential Seal, Palestine and all 50 states. Our church is charismatic, and because charismatics look at the ceiling of their auditoriums more than anywhere else, we hung the flags from the ceiling as a constant reminder to the congregation of the reason we do what we do in our living room: others, not ourselves.

In addition, we are currently building The World Prayer Center directly in front of our building. This center will gather information on Church growth from all around the world and feed that information to intercessors. The purpose is to keep the intercessors of the world praying for the lost, and to provide them with feedback information so they know that their prayers are being answered. Because the kind of praying that emanates from there is for the expansion of God's kingdom, and for the continued outpouring of the Holy Spirit worldwide, the World Prayer Center is a symbol of evangelistic prayer. We want everyone who drives into our church parking lot to be reminded to pray for the lost and to focus their attention on others rather than themselves.

OUR JERUSALEM

The first step in helping our congregation to become aware of outreach is to lead people in praying for their "Jerusalem," Colorado Springs. We often distribute a copy of the obituaries to each member of the New Life staff on a paper that says, "Today some people from Colorado Springs will be going to Heaven and some will be going to Hell. Our work today will affect the percentage going to Heaven or Hell tomorrow."

We pray through the phone book, over maps and for other churches. We pray for government leaders, schools and neighborhoods. And, probably the most effective way we help our congregation touch the lost of our city is by having them prayerwalk our city.

We coordinate our prayerwalking efforts with scores of other local churches to ensure that every street in the entire city is prayerwalked at least once a year.

One night my friend and I were prayerwalking through downtown Colorado Springs at about 1:30 in the morning. We were walking on a bridge high over some railroad tracks when we heard a noise on the tracks below. We leaned over the edge and saw a group of skateboarders playing on the concrete beneath the bridge. I yelled in the gruffest voice I could muster, "Hey you boys! What are you doing down there?"

The students looked up and, after a pause, one of them sheepishly questioned, "Pastor Ted, is that you?"

I was shocked! After composing myself and feeling a little embarrassed, I acknowledged to this young man, playing with his buddies in the middle of the night, that his senior pastor from the church in the suburbs was downtown playing too. My friend and I walked down to the railroad tracks to speak with them. It turned out that the boy from our church had slipped out of his bedroom window without his parents' knowledge so he could meet his buddies. And wouldn't you know it, his senior pastor showed up! How do you explain that to Mom at breakfast?

PRAYERWALKING CAUSES THE PEOPLE OF OUR CHURCH TO TOUCH, SEE, SMELL AND FEEL OUR COMMUNITY AT LARGE; IT MAKES US WANT TO SERVE OTHERS, NOT JUST OUR OWN LITTLE WORLD.

As it turned out, the boy told his parents, and his mom and dad were very grateful. Sadly, several months later his mom died and I was asked to participate in the funeral. Because of our meeting under the bridge, this young man and I were unusually connected, which made the struggle of burying his mother much easier for both of us. We weren't strangers, nor were we limited to our church roles, because of prayerwalking. Prayerwalking got me into his world so I became human, and I hope, a friend.

Similar stories are often told around our church. We have prayerwalking teams that target schools, certain businesses, teenage hangouts, government buildings, high places, power points and occult sites. Sometimes we prayerwalk a geographical area, and other times we strategically target a site or series of sites. Either way, prayerwalking causes the people of our church to touch, see, smell and feel our community at large; it makes us want to serve others, not just our own little world.

Therefore, some of our missions money goes to our Jerusalem. We give to various community organizations that serve our community in Jesus' name. We don't have to create any organizations ourselves, instead we partner with those that already exist but need financial assistance. Incidentally, I make a point of financing neighboring organizations with no strings attached. I don't want to serve on their boards or organize their ministries, I just want our church to help them fulfill their calling, thus our Jerusalem is moving a little more in the right direction.

OUR JUDEA

The second charge of the Great Commission is our Judea, which is to us our state, or our nation. Several years ago the Lord spoke to me and told me to send prayer teams to every county seat in the state of Colorado. As a result of that effort, our church has enjoyed expanded relationships with churches throughout our state. Not only have many of our counties improved spiritually, but members of our congregation have connected with counties outside their normal sphere of influence and, in many cases, developed a heartfelt concern for others.

OUR SAMARIA

The next groups are outside our region: "Samaria, and to the ends of the earth." In Jesus' day, Samaria was a despised group of people from the north of Judea. When Jesus said that the power of the Holy Spirit would give His disciples power to be witnesses in Samaria, He was sending them with the gospel to people of a different culture. To do this, we send people in our congregation on prayer journeys and in a few cases, to be missionaries in the traditional sense.

In my experience, prayer journeys are the most effective way to expose the people within our congregations to the mission field. Training is unnecessary in cross-cultural communications, witnessing, conducting services or any of the other issues that would otherwise cause people to be hesitant to go. Instead, prayer journeys enhance their prayer lives. People begin praying together with others from their home church; they practice by participating in prayerwalking in their own community; then they travel and pray for those living in a dark region of the world.

I enjoy prayer journeys not only because they always open the door for powerful spiritual advances, but also because they are fun. They have been packed with adventure and are too numerous to recount in detail within the pages of this short chapter. We have prayed through caves lined with bloody altars that have been used to sacrifice animals for more than 1,500 years; prayed through secret underground prisons once used by the communists; and stood on the dome of Islamic Mosques with both arms raised, claiming the building and the Islamic worshipers for Christ.

Perhaps I should take the time to tell about slipping through the dark streets in the capitals of closed Islamic nations to meet secretly with members of the underground church in order to train them in warfare prayer. There was also the time God supernaturally opened the clouds so our helicopter could seemingly appear out of nowhere to pluck our prayer team off the top of a mountain just in time.

Maybe it would be more interesting if I wrote about the prayer journeyer who was supernaturally protected from being hit by a bus that might have killed her without divine intervention, or the team members who were praying in tongues in an Islamic hospital only to discover that the patients understood them and started speaking back to them in their own language, just as in the book of Acts. The supernatural physical miracles that took place among the patients in that hospital didn't just lead to the healing of the patients, but also to the conversion of many doctors and nurses who were treating them. These high-adventure experiences are some of the reasons why prayer journeys are motivating for the people of our churches.

Prayer journeys are the penetration of God's commando forces—that's you and me, and the people of our churches—into enemy territory. I've led teams to the heart of Islam, Buddhism, Hinduism and other non-Christian religions. Why? Because I don't want even one more barrel cast into the sea.

We have watched too many people bow to Mecca, burn incense, dip in rivers, slaughter animals and construct idols only to have them become worse off after their futile attempts to find God. To cancel the effects of demonic opposition and open the windows of heaven, prayer must be the number one charge. Prayer is the way to produce a global impact.

Then we follow with strategic evangelism. In one of the nations we targeted with prayer, the Body of Christ grew 600 percent during the 12 months that followed; the growth rate the next year was 300 percent. In another nation we targeted for prayer, the underground church was soon networked, mobilized and trained to pray through the homes, recreation sites and worship sites of its Islamic masters. We are trusting God for revival there. In our most recent "target" nation, the Body of Christ is doubling every year! Prayer journeys combined with strategic partnerships for evangelism produce tangible results, every time.

The mission statement of our outreach office "is to spiritually and financially support, equip and empower missionaries and national workers who serve primarily in the 10/40 Window and among the least evangelized people groups."

To do this, we begin with a strategy. We want to touch those areas of the world that have the greatest need and, at the same time, have fertile spiritual soil. If they are hard, we send prayer teams. If they are prepared for evangelism, we send prayer teams and develop alliances with organizations or churches that already have some work in the region we can support.

"10/40 WINDOW"

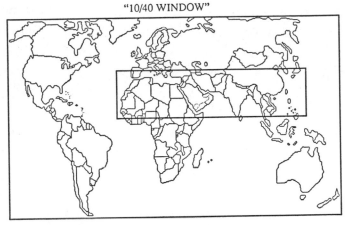

For example, in 1993 Albania was a predominantly Islamic nation ripe for the gospel. New Life Church sent our prayer team there, along with many other teams from other organizations, and enjoyed great encouragement from the Lord about the prospects for the Church among the Albanian people. Thus, upon our return home, we partnered with Every Home for Christ and the Gideons. We didn't have much financial strength at the time, so we made arrangements with both of these organizations to work through them in Albania. As a result, the kingdom of God received much greater strength through partnering than we could have ever have achieved working independently.

Currently, I believe Nepal is ready for revival. So, New Life Church is working in Nepal through five organizations that were already making headway there. We haven't had to train missionaries, buy land, build anything, hire anyone or fly anyone over there. Instead, we are working through organizations we know and trust that already have an infrastructure in place. As a result, we are seeing great results from our investment for the kingdom of God.

Strategy and partnership are the two strongest ideas behind our missions philosophy. In order to be strategic, we focus our efforts on the least evangelized people in the world. And to maximize effectiveness, we never launch into projects alone. New Life Church always partners with other ministries, such as Youth

With A Mission, Every Home for Christ, International Bible Society and others, or trustworthy national brethren. With the combination of being strategic and multiplying our efforts through partnerships, we have been able to maximize our impact among some of the most difficult to reach areas of the world.

I am writing this chapter today in Denver, Colorado, where I just finished a meeting with Eric Watt, missions strategist for the Christian Broadcasting Network; Charles Blair from Calvary Temple in Denver; Howard Foltz from AIMS; and about a half dozen leaders of networks of churches. We were developing strategy that would incorporate literature distribution, church planting and media efforts among unreached people groups. Together, we are all more effective than we ever could be alone.

When we consider training or sponsoring missionaries, we want to know:

1. Are they strategic in their thinking and planning? We recognize that every place has need, but is their destination a location of particular darkness, and are they the best resource we can send to penetrate that darkness?
2. Are they interested in training and enabling national workers to reach their own people? There is some value in direct cross-cultural ministry, but any value that is there impacts the culture most and continues multiplying for years if it includes training and empowering nationals to work within their own culture.

Once we have decided to support a missionary, we have certain guidelines that keep the relationship healthy. They are as follows:

- We don't support more than 35 percent of any missionary's total income. The only exception is if the missionary comes from our church. Then, we will support that person 100 percent for the first two years to give them time to build a support base. After two years, we limit our giving to 35 percent.

- We send all missions support on a monthly basis whether the money is sent to a missionary or to an organization that we are partnering with on a specific target.
- Occasional one-time gifts toward specific efforts and projects are given.
- Our missions-support structure is simple. At the end of every year, we review the amounts and the ministries of everyone receiving missions support. We decide to either increase, decrease or eliminate their support at the end of each year.
- Then we have a balance of how much more we want to commit to missions for the next year. At that time, we review all the applications and opportunities we have received from the previous year and decide which new projects or people we will agree to help for the following calendar year.
- Some of the selection criteria we use include:
  a. Personal integrity of character;
  b. Established work;
  c. Good stewardship of gifts and funds;
  d. Personal relationship with the senior pastor or missions director.

Once a missionary or project is on the support list, we maintain simple but informative communication with them so those on the field can spend their time doing mission work and we at home can spend our time strengthening the Church here.

INVESTING FOR FUTURE IMPACT

I believe one of the reasons families enjoy raising their children at New Life is because of our missions emphasis. Our church has a very distinct missions philosophy that purposefully directs the young people of our church.

Our newborn through fifth-grade children's cells emphasize primary Bible education, which consists of basic Bible stories. We tell the stories of the Bible again and again, in every possible way. Many of our children's cells are held in bright rooms with puppets, actors and sometimes popcorn. We provide maps, globes, missionaries and every possible tool to communicate the gospel message. We tell Bible stories, act them out, draw them and sing them. We use every method we can think of to tell Bible stories to this age group.

Sixth through eighth-grade cells emphasize secondary application. We teach how the Bible applies to the lives of young people in this age group. In other words, we explain that because Abraham did this, we need to do it, too. Or because Paul said this, so must we. Our goal is that the Bible becomes personal and powerful in the daily lives of our youth. The middle-school meetings and cells all focus on learning and applying the Scriptures.

Ninth through twelfth grades teach personal purpose and local church participation with a global perspective. This group emphasizes the compelling call and purpose from God for every student's life.

In these cells, the emphasis is our personal role in the global church. We try to take at least 100 of these high school students overseas every year. To stimulate a global conscience, they carry passports to their meetings and receive encouragement to discuss the condition of the Church in various parts of the world. They understand that God has called them to global evangelization. We teach them strategy, city-reaching techniques, intercessory prayer, warfare prayer, networking, evangelism, and prayer and fasting.

This group is the fertile soil into which we plant seeds of loving leadership to produce a crop of Christian leaders who will love the local church and understand its role in the global church. These students learn holiness, calling, purpose, dying and anointing. Most churches retain about 30 percent of their high school graduates for the kingdom of God by the time they graduate from college; New Life retains more than 95 percent because of its global emphasis.

Our college meetings and cells deal with strongholds. This group tackles the major economic, theological and philosophical issues of our day and learns the Christian worldview in response. They are learning to pull down strongholds in people's minds. They are preparing to enter into adult life and either become missionaries or support missions for the rest of their lives because, after all, they are from a life-giving church, which means they are called to have a global impact.

Life-giving churches make it hard for God's children of every age to forget the bravery and sacrifice of those who have given all to lead a lost and dying world back to the giver of all life, Jesus Christ. They make it hard to forget that God gives us His life so we can be His life givers "in Jerusalem, and in all Judea and Samaria, and to the ends of the earth."

10

Impartation of Life: Worship

By Ross Parsley, Worship Pastor

LET THE WORD OF CHRIST DWELL IN YOU RICHLY
AS YOU TEACH AND ADMONISH ONE ANOTHER WITH
ALL WISDOM, AND AS YOU SING PSALMS, HYMNS
AND SPIRITUAL SONGS WITH GRATITUDE IN YOUR
HEARTS TO GOD. AND WHATEVER YOU DO,
WHETHER IN WORD OR DEED, DO IT ALL IN
THE NAME OF THE LORD JESUS, GIVING THANKS
TO GOD THE FATHER THROUGH HIM.

[*Colossians 3:16,17*]

THE WORSHIP LIFE

Life-giving worship is not just singing, nor is it a three-song warm-up for the sermon. Life-giving worship doesn't only happen when we gather for Sunday services, nor is it an event; it's our lifestyle.

When we define worship as devoting our time, attention and affection to Him, every area of our lives is involved. Playing with our kids, encouraging friends, working conscientiously, and gathering together with other believers to sing, read the Word and express our love for God and one another are all forms of worship.

Jesus said the Father is seeking those who will worship in Spirit and truth. We worship in Spirit through our communication and relationship with Him. And we worship in truth as we authentically reflect who He is in us to others. Our goal then is to have a constant demonstration of His presence in our lives so others can join with us. This is the foundation upon which life-giving praise and worship is built.

THE WORSHIP LEADER

Worship is a high and holy calling. Every believer is called to be a worshiper. But when called to lead others into worship, we have an added responsibility. We must evaluate whether our hearts are pure, wholly submitted to Him and focused on glorifying Him.

Our motives and intentions need to be scrutinized as we consider what an honor and privilege it is to administrate the worship of others' hearts toward God. As we embrace this calling, it quickly becomes evident that if we ever treat worship as a hobby or something routine, God will replace us.

He is life, and worship to Him brings life. In order to keep worship from being polluted, God must graciously mold His worship leaders into holy vessels. He wants worshipers to receive His life as they worship Him, life Himself.

Our first responsibility as life-giving worship leaders is to minister to the Lord. Jesus is the center of attention at all life-giving services. There is no other good reason for us to gather than to meet with Him and study His Word. Without the Lord as our primary focus, we become ritualistic and social, but with Him at the center of attention, we are able to minister life to those around us.

Worship is not a monologue, it is a dialogue. It's not telling God what we think of Him, or giving Him a laundry list of what we want from Him. Praise and worship begins a spiritual dialogue through which He breathes His life into our hearts and minds, which conforms us into His image. As we engage in this wonderful conversation, the Lord imparts His heart, which leads to conviction, revelation and intercession. God's heart is fixed on rescuing the lost, and when we worship Him, our focus shifts from ourselves to others; consequently, we are led to intercede and work to reach others.

Jesus said, "the Son of Man did not come to be served, but to serve, and to give his life as a ransom for many" (Matt. 20:28; Mark 10:45). Musicians find it easy to get sidetracked and concentrate on performance, talent or personal recognition. However, our attitudes need to be the same as that of Christ Jesus who laid down His rights, His reputation and His preferences in order to take on the nature of a servant to all humankind.

As musical servants to the Body of believers, we must give up our rights, our agendas and our preferences so we can concentrate on the Lord's purposes. We don't sing and play our instruments to be served and seen, but to serve and give our lives for others.

That's why we worship, not just in our hearts but with our lives as well. Worship is a physical demonstration of the spiritual realities in our hearts. Just as communion reminds us of Christ's body and blood, and water baptism is where we identify with Christ's death, burial and resurrection, so our physical actions in praise and worship reflect the surrendering of our hearts to God.

When we praise the Lord with clapping, singing, shouting, dancing, lifting our hands, kneeling, bowing or standing, we are demonstrating with our bodies what our spirits already know: God is absolutely worthy of our praise. We demonstrate through our bodies His truth in our hearts. These physical manifestations of praise are the gateway for releasing our spirits to worship God. When we make our bodies serve our hearts, we fulfill the command to love God with all our hearts, minds, souls and strength.

Just as we use our bodies to demonstrate worship, we can also use our emotions for worship. God is emotional. If you doubt it, just read the Old Testament. He created us in His image and wants us to interact with Him in an emotional way.

Many people think that emotionalism is defined as showing a lot of emotion. But, the true definition of emotionalism is allowing our emotions to dictate our actions. We don't do that. Instead, we allow the realities of eternal life to dictate our worship. We worship, no matter what our emotions are. Often deciding to worship first results in becoming joyous or contemplative, but we worship.

One of the best examples of a passionate worshiper is King David, writer of the Psalms. Many times David used his emotions as the impetus for worshiping God. No matter what frame of mind he was in, David did not allow his emotions to determine his response to God. Instead, he used his emotions to press in to meeting with God. When David was sad, he found hope in God. When he was afraid, he ran to God for refuge. When he was grateful, he declared the greatness of God. Regardless of circumstances, David found the place of worship each time. He knew how to encourage himself in the Lord, because no matter how he felt, David understood the truth of God's worthiness and His faithfulness to him (see Ps. 42).

David not only modeled for us the way to worship in the midst of various emotions, he also modeled humility in worship. Throughout the Bible we see God resisting the proud and giving grace to the humble. Have you ever wanted to do something in praise and worship but didn't because you were embarrassed? Have you ever heard others talk about the depth of their personal worship experience or the freedom for worship in their local church with just a subtle hint of arrogance?

Our focus in worship should never be ourselves, and yet too many times in our own minds we become the central issue during worship. Whether it's feeling unworthy or just unruly, in order to worship, we must take our eyes off of ourselves or what others may think, and fix them upon the true subject of our worship, Jesus.

The more I realize that worship is a gift God grants me by His grace, the more that realization makes me want to capitalize on every opportunity to worship Him. Romans 11:36 says, "For him and through him and to him are all things." This is central to understanding our position in worship. The desire is *for Him*; the ability and gifting come *through Him*; and our purpose is to bring all the glory back *to Him*.

THE WORSHìP TEAm

Leading worship requires both heart and skill. Clean hearts are essential to successfully leading others to the life of God. Worship is a heart connection with God that relies upon the transparency and vulnerability of our hearts when we come to Him. This is important for leaders to understand, because our primary responsibility is to model openness of heart as we stand before the Body of believers.

Skill, on the other hand, has to do with our God-given abilities to accomplish what He has called us to do through music.

Music, just like preaching or plumbing, has an element of skill-fulness that either increases or decreases our effectiveness with others. The parable of the talents illustrates for us that we are stewards responsible to cultivate the gifts or talents we have received. When we don't, we are called lazy and wicked servants. Yikes!

With the privilege of leading worship comes the responsibility to develop our craft; however, we must keep the motivation pure. Excellent music on its own will not do anything eternal for our souls, but meeting with Jesus changes us every time. Therefore, excellence is only useful in our music for one reason: to provide an atmosphere for people to enter into God's presence, free from distractions. Great music under the inspiration of the Holy Spirit is an unparalleled combination to lead people into His presence.

Every one of us influences those around us. We are all leaders. The choir is not the background for the leader. The band does not just accompany the person in front. We don't have backup singers; we are all worship leaders. As worship leaders, we live worship, always. We sing with a purpose because we have a responsibility as leaders to be prepared, both musically and spiritually. When we stand before the congregation, we are the instruments of the Holy Spirit to inspire, motivate and encourage hearts to enter into worship. Each of us must embrace the idea that we are accountable to the Lord for this ministry, which causes us to be leaders who are motivated, instead of just participants depending on someone else.

Auditions

So why can't just anyone be on the platform? Are auditions OK?

Yes, auditions are OK, really! Heart attitude and various ability levels are the reason we need an audition process for the music ministry. Everyone cringes at the thought of auditions, but we don't intimidate people, we help them to discern where God wants to use them in their gifts. If leading others in praise and worship is a high and holy calling, then there should be some prayerful consideration given as to who should be involved.

Psalm 66:1 says, "Make a joyful noise unto God" (Ps. 66:1, *KJV*), and this exhortation is completely appropriate for every believer. But when we aspire to stand before the Body and inspire worship in others, we have to balance the desire of our hearts with our talents for specific roles within the Body. Luke 12:48 says, "From everyone who has been given much, much will be

———

IN THE PROCESS OF FINDING OUR ROLES
WITHIN THE BODY, WE MUST NEVER CONFUSE
WHAT WE DO WITH WHO WE ARE.

———

demanded; and from the one who has been entrusted with much, much more will be asked." Every one of us has been given much, and God expects us to work within the Body to find the area where we can best serve. For those who have musical skills that are recognized by others, the Bible says, "Sing to him a new song; play skillfully, and shout for joy" (Ps. 33:3).

As the music pastor, the Lord has given me the responsibility and spiritual authority to assist Him in inviting people to join the worship ministry in our local church. With this understanding, I ask each person to trust God and to trust me in helping to find his or her best place of ministry in the church. Therefore, when I don't invite people to be part of the worship leadership team, I believe I am encouraging them to discover the place where their giftedness will better serve the Body in order to release the fullness of God's call in their lives.

In the process of finding our roles within the Body, we must never confuse what we do with who we are. Musicians are a strange breed. I know because I am one. We are very creative, sensitive and emotional people, who at times wear our feelings on our sleeves. We often confuse who we are with what we do because our music is such a deep expression of our lives. But if we never learn to separate the two, we set ourselves up for heartbreak.

The truth is that we are all children of God created in His image. We are all the righteousness of God in Christ, and we are all citizens of heaven. This is who we are.

The gifts God has given us are His. They are simply what we do in the Body, not who we are to Him. We don't rely on our roles to give us worth or to make us feel as though we have significance. We don't use our gifts for the prestige or the applause of people. When we separate what we do from who we are, then we can allow others to speak into our lives, to give us direction, to properly place us according to our talents and the needs within our churches, and to instruct us and make us better at what we do.

If we do not separate these issues in our lives, then we become resistant, controlling, obstinate and proud, or we move in the other direction and become too timid or threatened to try. Yes, it is possible for us to both submit our gifts and talents to the Lord, and to allow others to input into our lives to make us more effective in the kingdom of God. When we do this, we stay humble, openhanded and can be a blessing to everyone.

The basis for the team relationship as well as the audition process is Ephesians 4:15 where Paul tells us to speak the truth in love so we can all grow in Christ. Mature relationships require the truth, but not the truth without love.

Usually we either get the ooey-gooey love with no truth, or the brutal truth without love. You may have heard the saying

People don't care how much you know, until they know how much you care. Consider that quote when interacting with musicians. They will respond positively, even to difficult news, if they know that you care about them, if they know you have the courage to shoot straight with them, and if they see your willingness to take the time to invest in them. It's hard work, but well worth the investment.

Rehearsals

Music is the tool to help people worship Him. If the music is not well done, it becomes distracting. If it is well done, people don't notice either those of us who are leading or the music; they notice Him instead, and that is our goal.

Oh, I know it's easy to get bogged down in all the work of rehearsals and preparation and planning, but we do it for a higher purpose. The rehearsals are important because the better we are rehearsed, the easier it is to use the tool of music to encourage worship in others. The sharper the ax, the faster the tree falls, but remember...the music rehearsal is only the tool being sharpened for the greater assignment. The reason for learning music and working hard is so we can internalize the message and be free to embrace the bigger picture of what we do.

Our purpose is bigger than Sunday morning. The reason for having a choir is not the choir. The reason for our church is not the church itself. The reason we're here is that vast numbers of lost people within our city need the power and presence of God in their lives. The ministry exists so they will meet Him.

Once the worship team, choir or orchestra is formed, that group must mold into a family of worshipers. The praise and worship ministry is both outward and inward in its focus and function. Our primary responsibility is to lead the congregation into His presence. At the same time, we must invest in one another and develop relationally so we can become a healthy, vibrant Body of believers.

Cells

To strengthen the interpersonal connections within the worship team, New Life's praise and worship ministries function as a section within the cell system. We have cells entitled Basic Music Stuff, Children's Choir, Youth Choir, Choir, three Exploring Worship cells, a Learning to Sing cell, a Prayer Team for Worship Ministries cell, etc. Through these cells we develop the relationships that keep people connected as a body, as a family of worshipers.

Each cell is a family within a family, and we treat each other as such. Singing with a bunch of people you don't know is neither powerful nor dynamic. But when you've developed a bond of relationships and experiences, worship comes alive.

Our effectiveness in leading worship is genuinely increased when surrounded by people we know, love and trust. When we're connected to each other, we play better, we sing better and we minister with more confidence and authority. After all, relationships are what we're all about, loving God and loving people.

Because of this structure and philosophy, it's easy to embrace the team mentality. As the music pastor, I am the section leader over all the worship cells and the cell leader over the choir. Because I have the heart of a pastor, I love doing what I do with the team. I wouldn't want to do it by myself. An understanding of team dynamics is essential to effective music ministry, and a requirement for receiving God's blessing.

Psalm 133:1,3 says, "How good and pleasant it is when brothers live together in unity!...For there the Lord bestows his blessing, even life forevermore." These verses highlight the pleasure the Lord receives when we live and work together for a common purpose. The team mentality requires everyone to give up their rights as individuals for the good of the whole. We surrender ourselves to bigger goals and objectives, and because we are teammates, we each fulfill our different roles, allowing God to use us as one.

Our numbers provide strength, both physical and spiritual. Of course, this means that we have no tolerance for hot shots or prima donnas. But when we serve each other in humility, then together we accomplish more than we ever could on our own. When we flow together in unity, we get stronger anointing, greater power and most importantly, God's blessing.

THE WORSHIP SERVICE

Two major ingredients for a life-giving church service are corporate worship and the public reading of Scripture.

We come together to give our hearts to the Lord, to minister to one another and to share the Word, all in the context of worship. We attend God. We celebrate His attributes. We worship His majesty, and our hearts are changed in His presence. This is who we are and what we do as believers.

When the life of God is flowing, there should be lots of smiling and laughing. People should be relaxed and feel at home. I'm convinced many people have difficulty enjoying church, simply because they take themselves too seriously. The reason we go to church is to enjoy being with God and with other believers as we function as his Body. There is great delight in that.

A life-giving worship service should feel like a gathering of friends. You know, like when the family is having dinner together and there's a roar of conversation and laughter. People who always approach God with a wrinkled forehead and tight hair miss out on the joy and pleasure of being with the family of believers in worship. Take a drink of living water. Enter into His rest and enjoy Him. And whatever you do, don't become so serious that you lose sight of why you're there.

I was in a church not long ago where the senior pastor was not even in the auditorium during the praise and worship. Then, toward the end of the worship time, he was ushered into the room. While the worship was finishing, he was reading his Bible and seemed to be waiting for worship to finish.

I'm confident that this brother loves to worship the Lord. But his actions came across to me a little self-absorbed and rude to the worship leader. He was reading while others were worshiping, communicating that the worship was to prepare the crowd for the main event, his sermon. It made me appreciate the norm in most life-giving churches, where the senior pastor understands his role in loving the worship leader and helping him lead the congregation in worship.

NOT ONLY DO PEOPLE LOOK *TO* THEIR SENIOR PASTOR FOR THE VISION OF THE CHURCH, BUT THEY LOOK *AT* HIM DURING SERVICES TO SEE HIS VISION FOR WORSHIP.

It is wonderful when the senior pastor has the heart and passion for leading the church by example in worship. As the one who has been given the spiritual authority to lead the local church, the senior pastor communicates the vision and direction for everything from style to our theology of worship. Not only do people look *to* their senior pastor for the vision of the church, but they look *at* him during services to see his vision for worship.

The worship leader might be trying to lift the people to a higher place in worship, but they won't go unless the senior pastor models worship in his lifestyle. When people see their senior pastor abandoning himself in freedom to praise God wildly, and to worship God in humility, they follow him.

As the spiritual leader, the senior pastor profoundly affects the focus and participation of everyone in attendance. So, senior pastors, lead on! It will be a great blessing to your church and especially to your worship leader.

Worship is making a heart connection. Preaching is not just for transferring information; it is connecting people's lives with the Word of God. The offering is not just a collection, but an act of worship. The singing of songs and our expressions of praise have one ultimate purpose: to open our hearts to the Holy Spirit's ministry and dialogue with us. This affects the kind of songs we choose, as well as the style and format we use to communicate them. Some people ask me, "Why do we have to sing these songs so many times through?"

My response is simple: Most of the time we don't grasp the concept or meaning of the songs until we've sung them a couple of times through, then we want to internalize them and use them to express our hearts to the Lord. Remember, the songs are not worship, but making a heart connection is!

What God thinks is most important. In the final analysis, what we think about our services is not the issue. When we step off the platform on Sundays, our observations of how people responded or what the tone of the meeting was or even how we *felt* about our "performance" are irrelevant. When all is said and done, it's what God thinks that counts.

No matter what happens musically or emotionally during a service, I have learned through experience that God gets the glory anyway. Again and again, I've finished a service that I thought was...let's say less than anointed, but when people approached me afterwards they have said, "That was the most anointed service I've ever been in. God met me and ministered to me in such a powerful way."

Then I think to myself, *Were you in the same service I was in?*

The point is this: Does God get the glory from our services, or do we shortchange Him by thinking it all depends on us? The answer is obvious. God's opinion is the final authority. We want Him to not only be pleased with us, but to receive glory from everything we do.

11

Integration of Life: Free Market Cells

With Russ Walker,
Pastor of Small Group Ministries

Get rid of all bitterness, rage and anger, brawling and slander, along with every form of malice. Be kind and compassionate to one another, forgiving each other, just as in Christ God forgave you

[*Ephesians 4:31,32*]

DISCIPLES, NOT SPECTATORS

Life-giving bodies of believers can thrive within any structure. They are found in networks of house churches as well as facility-based churches. Some are in denominations; others are independent. In North America, most churches are program based; internationally, most churches are cell based. Having a life-giving church is not contingent upon any particular structure or affiliation. The life of the church is based, instead, upon the spirit that operates within the group itself.

New Life Church represents an unusual combination of structures. I am a Southern Baptist pastor serving in an independent charismatic church. We as a church, though, are highly networked with other churches, locally, nationally and internationally. Our growth throughout the years, however, has dramatically changed the way we do church. We started as a home church, grew through a series of storefronts and became a facility-based program church. Now, as we've continued to grow, the church has become a facility-based cell church. In other words, we have great Sunday services that we all enjoy very much, but the majority of the pastoral care and discipleship occurs in the cells that are led by the ministers of our church, the laypeople.

When New Life was a program-based church, we had a series of departments that coordinated events. We, the paid pastoral team, taught, spoke and built the congregation. The church was relatively large, but we were impersonal in our structures. As we grew, we noticed that our systems were serving lots of people, but we were also beginning to hurt people by not genuinely connecting with them or aiding them in their development in ministry. This resulted in uncomfortably high flow-through. We realized that even though we appeared healthy, our programs produced too many spectators and not enough disciples.

Then it dawned on us: The largest churches in the world are cell churches. Asia, Africa and South America had the largest numbers of people in their churches, and they were empowering them to minister in small group ministries while we in North America were struggling to find a cell-church model that worked for us.

At New Life, we failed twice at adopting cell ministries into the life of our church. I had given up on cells when Larry Stockstill, the Pastor of Bethany World Prayer Center in Baker,

———

EVERYTHING GOD HAS DONE IN OUR LIVES IS UNPROVEN UNTIL IT IS REFINED AND DEMON-STRATED IN THE MIDST OF RELATIONSHIPS.

———

Louisiana, developed an extensive cell system that, though constantly evolving, was working. We sent our staff and key leaders to Bethany to learn. We liked what we saw. After working with the Bethany model for two years, we had 80 successful cells and were seeing positive results.

Larry Stockstill's book *The Cell Church* (Regal) explains the transition from a program-based church to a cell-based church better than any book I've seen. In the book, Brother Larry tells the story of how Bethany World Prayer Center transitioned to a cell church by observing the super megachurches of the world, and how each one ministered to its people and evangelized its community through cell groups.

I knew we had to restructure the way we grouped people so they could minister more effectively to each other. Obviously, being in a small group is the primary way we exemplify godliness.

Everything God has done in our lives is unproven until it is refined and demonstrated in the midst of relationships. There is no way to verify the work of His grace in us if we are independent of others; nor is there any way to demonstrate godliness to any other than God except through interaction with others.

PRESERVING THE LOCAL CHURCH

My difficulty was dealing with those who emphasize the role of small groups for enabling ministry without an adequate understanding of the vital role of the local church. I am an advocate of the local church. I believe in both the institution and its function. I never did, nor do I now, believe that the need for small groups should diminish or threaten the vital and irreplaceable role of strong, healthy local churches. Other groups, though, that emphasize the importance of weekend, facility-based, clergy-led worship services without productively linking believers together are just as problematic.

In the Early Church, even the participants of home meetings went to synagogue on a weekly basis, and still remained networked together through the council at Jerusalem. It seems that when alienation occurs at any level, the effectiveness of both the individual and the Body of Christ as a whole is limited.

I have become convinced that God is preparing to send revival. Therefore, we at New Life want the flexibility that cells provide so we can respond quickly to a rapid influx of new believers. We want to be structured to effectively train those who come to Christ. In our view, the best models for successfully discipling significant numbers of new believers are cell churches. We have noted, however, that even the most successful cell churches throughout the world have powerful weekend believers' meetings. The only exceptions are for obvious reasons in communist or Islamic countries. But in the rest of the world, strong facility-based ministries on weekends led by those who function in the ministry offices listed in Ephesians 4:11 are essential to the effective work of the church. The purpose, however, as I said earlier, is for the weekend meetings to equip all Christian people in their ministries so they can then minister in their homes and workplaces throughout the week (see Eph. 4:12,13).

A NEW REVELATION

Then, I began to experience a revelation in my spirit. Larry Stockstill's message about the necessity for cell churches in North America inspired me to strengthen the role of the believers who had spent years developing personal relationships and godly character in our congregation. I realized that the wisdom of age and the strength of personal example were not being adequately utilized, and too many church attendees were unnecessarily failing in their families and other areas of their lives. I had to do more. We had a successful church by most standards, but I knew we could do so much more if our Body could only connect. With our combined experience and insight, there was no reason for anyone in our Body to fail in any area of their lives.

Then a supernatural series of events started to occur. Almost every morning for a period of several weeks I woke up with a fresh thought about how cells could work in Colorado Springs, or new ideas would come to me during my prayer times. I formed special dream teams to help me think through the impact of the new simple system we were ready to launch. Every day we would meet to refine the ideas.

Rather than eliminating any of our existing programs, we decided to transition them into a new structure that would allow unlimited creativity and innovation. Thus we were able to unleash our Davids (see chapter 2) without threatening anyone. We didn't impose the transition to cells on the church; we offered it. Our cells were so appealing that the church naturally transitioned, and we didn't lose anyone from the church or from any of our old programs because we didn't eliminate anything. We simply gave our old programs opportunity to evolve, and people liked the improvements.

One Sunday morning before the early service, I was standing in my office worshiping when, in a split second, the Holy Spirit came upon me and changed me. I was the senior pastor of thousands of people, and God suddenly changed the purpose of the Sunday services. Rather than going to the service to teach First Peter, I was now going to the service to teach all of those attending to teach First Peter. I understood. Rather than teaching the life of Christ, I was to use the Sunday services to equip the congregation to teach the life of Christ. Sunday services had become in my heart the training, equipping and preparation meetings for empowering those people God had sent to New Life to multiply. Sunday services themselves became the training time for ministers.

Now Ephesians 4:11-16 made sense. Paul wrote:

It was he who gave some to be apostles, some to be prophets, some to be evangelists, and some to be pastors and teachers, to prepare God's people for works of service, so that the body of Christ may be built up until we all reach unity in the faith and in the knowledge of the Son of God and become mature, attaining to the whole measure of the fullness of Christ.

Then we will no longer be infants, tossed back and forth by the waves, and blown here and there by every wind of teaching and by the cunning and craftiness of men in their deceitful scheming. Instead, speaking the truth in love, we will in all things grow up into him who is the Head, that is, Christ. From him the whole body, joined and held together by every supporting ligament, grows and builds itself up in love, as each part does its work.

My understanding of my role was instantly transformed, and so were the roles of those who attended New Life Church. I was to be added to their ministries, they didn't have to be added to mine. They were the purpose; I was to train them. It was my job to build them up and equip them to do what God called them to do. I was their coach, their preparer, their enabler. I was to teach them to minister. I was to teach them First Peter so they could teach First Peter. I understood multiplication. I got it!

A NEW BEGINNING: FREE MARKET CELLS

Free Market Cells were born. Within two months the number of cells increased from 80 to 345. Three months later, that number grew to 392 cells—and it was easy. We didn't have to sell, negotiate with or pressure people. Instead, people joyfully participated because they knew that cells only lasted a semester, which gave them freedom to change groups as their interests or lives changed, and since they were grouped according to interest, stage of life or task, people could easily involve their friends.

Within weeks we offered cells based on books of the Bible, marriage, missions, parenting and prayer. Cells that study the previous week's sermon, emphasize the family, train men and network singles all formed naturally. Suddenly we had cells for children, homeschoolers, young people and women. Praise and Worship cells began training budding worshipers; outreach cells began creatively serving the lost; and recreational cells began connecting people from various backgrounds. Oral Roberts University now offers correspondence classes for credit toward a bachelor's degree through our cells!

Our menu of cells covers practically every interest, subject, profession and stage of life, and they flow naturally out of the congregation. That is what makes them easy. We don't have to think of topics and recruit people, the free market within the church does all of that work, which makes it fun and effective to train many more people in godliness than we ever projected.

THE FREE MARKET PARADIGM

How do we do it? Free markets allow people to be innovative and creative, like they were created to be. Countries that have free market economies allow their citizens the freedom to produce goods and services, and find the marketplaces full of products and their citizens well fed—Free Market Cells do the same thing. They allow people to be innovative and creative with ministry ideas, which keeps people spiritually well fed and growing because of the endless number of ministry opportunities.

All of our churches already have the internal resources to provide great ministries and receive the resulting benefits, and Free Market Cells provide simple tracks that enable people to minister the wisdom God has already built into their lives.

We've found that Free Market Cells work in every area of the church except the nurseries. No longer do cells need to be confined to home-fellowship meetings. With Free Market Cells, the cells are the church rather than being a church with cells. For example, no longer does our children's ministry function as a program of the church with its own recruitment and leadership development. Now each class is a children's cell, with the leadership receiving training through the cell ministry training that goes on for all the other cell leaders. We have now converted every area of New Life Church, from the choir to the youth ministries, to cells, restructuring the programs into small-group philosophy.

Last year New Life grew 24 percent. Our back door, the number of people who left the church, was only 7/10 of 1 percent. The low numbers leaving are attributed to Free Market Cells. They work so well that our new mission is to "promote healthy relationships through small groups, which empower people for ministry." Since we transitioned our children's ministry from Sunday School to children's cells, we not only have children's cells that meet in classrooms during regularly scheduled service times, but we also have children's cells meeting in apartment complexes, parks, daycare centers and homes. It's wonderful!

In the Free Market Cell model, the number of people in each group is not limited, but left to the ability of the leader and the interest of the people. Emphasis is given to attracting people to the cell through their felt needs, so a multitude of topics are available in the groups. People choose the kind of group they want to go to based on relationships or an interest or a need they might have. And, because Free Market Cells provide easy entrance and easy exit, people join cells without hesitation, knowing that every cell has a predetermined transition date, when either the cell ends and members of that cell find a new cell or decide to continue on the next semester with that same cell.

Because these groups are free market, the best groups are the ones that survive and multiply, creating other similar groups, while the weaker groups must improve to survive or dissolve.

Advantages to Free Market Cells

- All participants know in advance the length of time the group will meet so they can comfortably attend, knowing they can cycle out without rejecting anyone or having to quit.
- All groups attract participants through people they already know who have a common interest, or new people who are attracted because of the subject.
- Free Market Cells allow people with various gifts, talents, experiences and personality types to lead. This increases the leadership pool and causes diversity in styles of groups.
- Leaders can teach or lead the group in whatever topic they are most interested in at the time, causing leaders to stay for longer periods because they can switch subjects and styles of groups from semester to semester.

- Because the cells have a time line, some groups stay together and switch subjects each semester, while others continue with the same study. This gives the participants the freedom to transfer to other groups, and keeps the groups vital and constantly expanding.
- Interpersonal relationships remain as the groups evolve and multiply because the participants initially meet around a common interest.
- Groups multiply naturally without effort. Free Market Cells reward success by creating more cells like the successful ones.

The Threefold Purpose of Free Market Cells

1. *To build long-term healthy relationships between people.* The cell meeting is the launching pad people use to develop relationships. In the cell, members meet one another and have an opportunity to dialogue regularly. Because people join a cell based on a common felt need or interest, relationships are built naturally and quickly. Once this foundation is laid, the relationships begin to diversify outside of the scheduled cell meetings. Outside the cell, situations occur that, when properly coached, lead to genuine discipleship and spiritual growth throughout the cell. A sense of genuine community begins to be established and, as a result, the entire cell begins ministering to itself in a healthy way. This is when believers learn *to live* a righteous life, rather than just learning *about living* a righteous life. Cells cultivate a lifestyle of integrity rather than people who just believe they should have a lifestyle of integrity. Major difference.

2. *To disciple people until they become disciplers* (see Heb. 5:11—6:3). We call our cell leaders "life coaches" because they have a great opportunity to coach the people in their

cells in every area of life and to pull them up into ministry. Regardless of their cell subject, we train all of our life coaches how to role model, mentor, motivate and multiply themselves in every cell member. As a result, we have hundreds of people each week strengthening others. This system allows us to reach thousands on the weekends, and thousands more thoughout the week who do not come to our church but are positively impacted by those who do attend. Everyone is to disciple other people until they become disciplers. Multiplication. Major improvement, and much easier than our old system.

3. *To provide the unchurched a safe way to become associated with Christians.* We believe God has a calling on every person, whether they know it or not. Christian people know more about their callings than non-Christians do, so to help people find God's plan for their lives, we invite nonbelievers to our groups and, along with everyone else, they grow in the revelation of why God created us. We encourage every group member to invite an unchurched friend or relative to the group. And because of the structure of the group—common interests, clear purpose and limited duration—those who don't know Christ are very comfortable in these cells.

STRUCTURING THE CELL MINISTRY

The levels of leadership are: cell leader, Section leader, Zone leader and District leader. Each of these leaders is responsible for being life coaches to the people they serve:

- At least two people and one coach form a cell;
- Five to 12 cells form a Section;
- Five to 12 sections form a Zone; and
- Five to 12 zones form a District.

This is not a corporate organizational chart; it is a diagram of relationships that enable people in ministry. Therefore, staff members may be cell leaders, Section leaders, Zone leaders or District leaders. For example, I am a cell leader. I have a cell for ministry leaders that meets at 10:00 A.M. on Wednesday mornings. Pastors from other churches and leaders from servant ministries (parachurch ministries) attend. So the senior pastor is also a cell leader. I love it!

TYPES OF CELL GROUPS

Every ministry of the church, with the exception of the nursery, is a cell ministry. From our children's ministry to our senior's ministry, these cells serve our church and our city. They provide a place for anyone to be equipped to do works of ministry. As I mentioned earlier, not only are cells discussing my Sunday sermons—we call them sermon cells—but they also cover topics such as books of the Bible, various Christian books, marriage enrichment, biblical enrichment, biblical foundations and parenting.

We also have cells for specific groups of people: men, women, singles, seniors, handicapped and youth. In addition we have cell groups that accomplish a certain purpose: ushers, door greeters, musicians and children's workers. Furthermore, we have cell groups that get together for the purpose of doing a specific activity. For example, we have cooking, biking, quilting, various sports and a number of other activity cell groups. All of our cell groups have a purpose!—to help people grow in godliness around their interests.

Characteristics of a Free Market Cell
The following characteristics are the consistent elements included in all cell groups:

1. All cells must engage in one or more of the following:
   - Prayer
   - Worship

- Bible study
- Testimonies

2. All cells must welcome new people unless otherwise designated. For example, some of the marriage cells cannot be joined after they have begun.
3. All cells must have life coaches and assistant life coaches committed to providing pastoral-type support, equipping the cell members in spiritual growth, and intentionally empowering the people in their groups to be more successful in every area of their lives.
4. All cells are to develop members into future leaders.
5. All cell members are encouraged to bring unchurched people who have the same interest as the group within the first month of each new semester. The only exceptions are those groups that close to newcomers after the first week because of the nature of the cell.
6. All cells must have completed their study and be ready to either change subjects or receive additional people by the beginning of the next semester.
7. All cell leaders must communicate with their Section leaders weekly so the Section leaders can coach them for increasing effectiveness.
8. All cells must honorably reflect the ministry, spirit and theological position of New Life Church.

CELL-MINISTRY TRAINING

Three times a year we distribute sign-up cards throughout the congregation to encourage people to become cell leaders. These cards say that, to be a cell leader, a person must commit to:

1. Serve people;
2. Meet weekly with friends;

3. Receive initial training;
4. Get leadership coaching with the senior pastor;
5. Tithe.

If they are willing to do those five things, their next step is to attend an initial training class on a Sunday afternoon.

Training

1. Initial Training Class

The purpose of this class is to provide the future cell leader with the vision, purpose and structure of the cell ministry. Additional training is provided regarding small-group dynamics as well as training for each leader's specialized interests within the cell ministry (i.e., children's, music, Bible, sermons, etc.). These training classes are offered three times a year, approximately one month before the next semester begins on Sunday afternoons.

At the end of this class, applicants complete a form, indicating what topics they want to teach or facilitate. They are then interviewed by a Section leader and/or meet with a Zone leader or District pastor for approval. Once the topic or type of group has been approved, and the application has been approved, the person becomes a cell leader and his/her group will be listed on the menu for the next semester along with the appropriate information to advertise the group.

2. Weekly Leadership Training Class

Training takes place every Sunday night at 5:00 P.M., and every leader (cell leader, Section leader, Zone leader and District pastor) must attend this class. The purpose of this meeting is to provide ongoing leadership training for every leader in the church with the goal of improving their ministries to others. The senior pastor is primarily responsible for this training class; however, he may have a designated representative lead from time to time. The leadership training class format is as follows:

5:00 to 5:30 P.M.: Senior pastor or his representative will speak.

5:30 to 6:00 P.M.: Section leaders meet with their cell leaders (huddles).

5:30 to 6:00 P.M.: District leaders meet with their Zone leaders (huddles).

6:00 to 6:30 P.M.: Zone leaders meet with their Section leaders (huddles).

In addition, all leaders are to call their coaches once a week to give a report about their meeting(s). Thus, each person is in contact with the coach at least twice a week.

The Vital Link: Rally Week

To maintain continuity throughout the year, we use two Rally Weeks—one in January and the other in August—to launch the next semester's cells. Rally Week provides the focus, transition and entry points into cell groups. The Sundays prior to and following Rally Week are used to introduce the upcoming cell groups to the church. A menu with a list of all the cells is distributed in all services for an entire week. The menu includes the topic of each cell group, a brief description of the cell, a short profile about the person leading the group, and the day, time and location of the meeting. Unique characteristics are also listed such as possible costs involved (i.e., purchase of books or other materials), and whether childcare is provided or if a children's cell will coincide with the adult cell meeting. Rally Week consists of the following schedule:

Sunday A.M.: Explain the interrelationships among services, cells and our homes.

Sunday P.M.: Children's Rally Night

Monday: Men's Rally Night

Tuesday: Prayer and Outreach Night

CHAPTER ELEVEN

Wednesday: Ladies' Rally Night
Thursday: Music/Praise and Worship
Friday: Singles' Rally Night
Saturday Afternoon: 55 and Wiser Rally
Saturday Night: Youth Rally Night
Sunday A.M.: Commissioning Sunday
Sunday P.M.: Celebration!

At each of these rally-night meetings, we highlight various cells so people can learn more about what is available in their areas of interest. We advertise these rally-night meetings in the community. This system is exactly like the free market in that it looks like chaos, but under closer scrutiny, is systematically discipling believers who are connected with others. Mission accomplished.

12

Demonstration of Life: Elders

With Lance Coles, Pastor of Church Administration

Therefore I urge you to imitate me.

[*1 Corinthians 4:16*]

Defining the Role of the Elder

Several years ago I was at a pastors' retreat when the subject of church elders came up. Initial responses to the topic ranged from groans to stories of reckless disasters. It was interesting to me, though, that as pastors told stories about elders within their churches who had actually created problems rather than solved problems, each of them was quick to defend the biblical role of elders.

Because these pastors were from various styles of churches, their elders served in a variety of functions. The worst stories came from churches where elders managed rather than served the church, or where they tried to help in delicate situations in which they could not possibly understand the relational subtleties of their decisions, thus creating havoc.

Some would offer a defense of the faithful elders who serve in churches all around the world. The consensus was that most elders were fine people wanting to serve the Body, but that they were poorly placed in structures that put them in situations unsuitable for their experience.

As part of this discussion, I presented the difference between the corporate and the spiritual functions of our churches, and asked whether their elders served spiritual roles, corporate roles, or both. Every one of them said both. I asked if they thought that was the problem. They thought it was. I asked for any suggestions, they had none.

But I did!

This chapter on the role of elders is just that—a suggestion. It's the way we structure the elders ministry at New Life and in our sister churches; it works well. I know that life-giving churches throughout the world structure the function of elders differently, and I'm not suggesting this is the way life-giving churches should operate. As a matter of fact, I'm convinced there is no "absolutely correct" way. But I do believe some structures are more helpful to effective ministry than others.

Our elders don't have any corporate power. On the chart of the corporate and the spiritual, our elders serve the spiritual Body of believers. Their role is to help the senior pastor and his staff keep the church spiritually healthy. They have well-defined functions they perform to keep our Body stable and consistent.

As all Christian leaders know, seemingly endless discussion continues about the title and role of elders. Therefore, the title has evolved to identify various offices and functions within the church, depending on the church's interpretation of Scripture and history. Despite these variations, though, individuals who either perform the function or are placed in the office of elder should always meet the biblical requirements for eldership:

> An elder must be blameless, the husband of but one wife, a man whose children believe and are not open to the charge of being wild and disobedient. Since an overseer is entrusted with God's work, he must be blameless—not overbearing, not quick-tempered, not given to drunkenness, not violent, not pursuing dishonest gain. Rather he must be hospitable, one who loves what is good, who is self-controlled, upright, holy and disciplined. He must hold firmly to the trustworthy message as it has been taught, so that he can encourage others by sound doctrine and refute those who oppose it (Titus 1:6-9).

Now, with 2,000 years of development since these Scriptures were written, elders fill three dominant roles for various groups.

Overseers
The first group oversees churches from outside the local Body. Some would call this group elders, others call them apostles, pres-

byters, bishops or denominational overseers. I call the outside group of elders who oversee churches overseers. Their purpose and authority are described in Article Eight of our Bylaws.

Pastors

The second group of elders is comprised of the pastoral team in a local church. Because of the nature of their roles, we believe the pastoral team should serve and be recognized as the elders who manage the day-to-day operation of the local church. To avoid confusion with the third group of elders, we refer to them as pastors, but often emphasize their ability and responsibility to also serve as elders.

Elders

The third group is the subject of this chapter. They consist of men and women within our local churches who meet the qualifications for an elder and are recognized by the congregation as functioning in that capacity, but they earn their living in the community, not from the tithes of the church members. In our church, they are able to function as elders once elected by the church Body.

In our church government, even though overseers, pastors and elders all meet the biblical qualifications for elders, we have distinguished these three roles with distinct functions. As I've already mentioned, the function of the overseers is described in Article 8 of our Bylaws and the functions of the pastors are discussed in various chapters of this book. Now let's discuss the functions of the elders.

Ten Unique Roles of the Elders

Those we call elders have 10 unique roles they fulfill within our church policy, as outlined in Article Nine of our Bylaws. Even though these elders must perform many more functions within the Body to serve it effectively, the following are identified as the 10 essential to the effective flow of ministry to the church.

I. Teach by Living a Godly, Christian Lifestyle

Elders should reflect a Christlike lifestyle that maintains the respect and confidence of the people whom they serve. We ask our elders to:

- Be responsible financially by living within their means. This idea includes prompt payment of all financial obligations, support of the church and faithfully caring for their families so they can model wise financial planning.
- Avoid the appearance of evil in every area of their lives, which means elders must be careful of what they watch, what they drink, their speech, how they dress, and every other attitude and action. This, too, is a stabilizing force within the church Body as the elders model mature Christian living.
- Demonstrate personal discipline. Personal habits, proper hygiene, appropriate dress and control of eating and exercise all model healthy Christian living for others.
- Show wisdom in their ability to bring others to maturity by successfully participating in the small-group ministries of the church.

We don't want to list every detail of what a godly Christian lifestyle is, and we certainly don't want to fall into the trap of policing others, but this list gives the elders an idea of what kinds of things are important in modeling godliness.

II. Provide a Prayer Shield for the Pastoral Team and the Local Church

Every Christian needs a prayer shield, but because pastors and other Christian leaders are at the spiritual hub of the church, they need even more spiritual protection than other members of the Body. The following reasons indicate why this may be so:

A. Pastors have more responsibility and accountability. James 3:1 says, "Not many of you should presume to be teachers, my brothers, because you know that we who teach will be judged more strictly."
B. Pastors are subjected to more temptation. Because a pastor's role requires that he be transparent and connect with people's hearts, he is subject to greater temptation than most.
C. Pastors are strategic targets for spiritual warfare. Servants of darkness single out pastors for their greatest onslaught of spiritual attack because they know that they can weaken thousands of Christians by getting just one leader to fall.
D. Pastors have more visibility. Because pastors are continually in the public eye, they remain under constant scrutiny and are too often the subject of gossip and criticism, which places an immense burden on them and their families.

Because of the responsibility to provide a prayer shield for the pastoral team and the church, we ask all of our pastors and elders to read and apply the principles in *Prayer Shield* (Regal) by Dr. C. Peter Wagner. This book is an excellent explanation of how to build protective prayer shields.

III. Defend, Protect and Support the Integrity of the Pastoral Team and the Local Church

Not only is the call to defend, protect and support the church and its leadership consistent with Titus 1:6-9, but this teaching is also consistent with James 3:5,6:

Likewise the tongue is a small part of the body, but it makes great boasts. Consider what a great forest is set on fire by a small spark. The tongue also is a fire, a world of evil among the parts of the body. It corrupts the whole person, sets the whole course of his life on fire, and is itself set on fire by hell.

Elders must always be conscious of their speech and not be silent in the face of verbal attacks against the pastoral staff or the local church. This means that elders are expected to speak proactively about the pastoral staff as well as the local assembly. Negative speech is like a cancer and once it spreads, it causes strife and a spiritually unhealthy Body.

I am not suggesting that any elder deny the reality of sin or abuse and ignore it. If for some unfortunate reason a just cause surfaces for criticism about the pastor, it should first be a matter of private prayer. If, after prayer, an elder discerns that pastoral discipline is necessary, then, the procedure is clearly outlined to confront the pastor under number IX of this chapter. But random discussions are not the way to correct problems, so the elders are to put out fires that might be in the congregation or community, and model wisdom in their speech.

IV. Pray for the Sick

The Bible is very specific about the role of prayer in the lives of the elders. James 5:14-16 says, "Is any one of you sick? He should call the elders of the church to pray over him and anoint him with oil in the name of the Lord. And the prayer offered in faith will make the sick person well; the Lord will raise him up. If he has sinned, he will be forgiven. Therefore confess your sins to each other and pray for each other so that you may be healed. The prayer of a righteous man is powerful and effective."

Elders are also included in the commission of the Lord Jesus when He commands all believers in Mark 16:18 to "place their hands on sick people, and they will get well." Clearly, Christ is the healer. Thus, the one who is laying hands on the sick person is an instrument through whom God's healing power can flow.

———

THE OUTCOME OF PRAYER IS NOT
DETERMINED BY A SPECIFIC FORMULA OR
APPLICATION, BUT BY GOD. THUS, THERE
IS NO PRESSURE ON THE ONE PRAYING
TO PERFORM A MIRACLE.

———

The outcome of prayer is not determined by a specific formula or application, but by God. Thus, there is no pressure on the one praying to perform a miracle.

Hospital Visitation Protocol

- Make sure the person in the hospital has requested or approves of receiving a visit.
- If someone else has requested a visit on behalf of the sick person, have the requesting party obtain permission from the patient or a family member (if the patient is not able) before the visit. This prevents the patient from being placed in the awkward situation of either having to tell you the visit is unwelcome, or being surprised when you drop in.
- If the patient does accept a visit that has been requested on his or her behalf, try to have the requesting party join you for the visit.

- Do not visit a young person or someone of the opposite sex alone. The exception might be an elderly person or a person with a terminal illness who has requested a private, personal meeting for spiritual reasons.
- Be patient and polite, not loud and self-righteous.
- Listen.
- Be encouraging and sensitive.
- Pray for and with the person, encouraging his or her personal relationship with the Lord.
- Do not attempt to give easy answers.

Procedures for Visitation

1. Before entering the room, ask God to anoint you with the power, wisdom and compassion of the Holy Spirit.
2. Ask the Lord for the gifts of healing and encouragement.
3. If the person doesn't know you, tell him/her who you are and that you are from the church.
4. Bring a gift, e.g., some candy, a Big Mac (if you know his or her diet allows it), a flower, or maybe a toy, a book or a knickknack to cheer up the room.
5. If other family members, friends or medical personnel are in the room, give them priority.
6. At the close of the visit, ask if you can help either the patient or that person's family in any way and follow through on your offer.
7. Convey your commitment to pray for the person and continue to offer support throughout their recovery.
8. Provide lots of opportunity for the patient to be exposed to the healing power of God's Word. The following are some verses you may want to share:

Exodus 15:26: "He said, 'If you listen carefully to the voice of the Lord your God and do what is right in his eyes, if you pay attention to his commands and keep all his decrees, I will not bring on you any of the diseases I brought on the Egyptians, for I am the Lord, who heals you.'"

Psalm 103:3: "Who forgives all your sins and heals all your diseases."

Isaiah 53:4,5: "Surely he took up our infirmities and carried our sorrows, yet we considered him stricken by God, smitten by him, and afflicted. But he was pierced for our transgressions, he was crushed for our iniquities; the punishment that brought us peace was upon him, and by his wounds we are healed."

Matthew 4:23: "Jesus went throughout Galilee, teaching in their synagogues, preaching the good news of the kingdom, and healing every disease and sickness among the people."

Matthew 8:16,17: "When evening came, many who were demon-possessed were brought to him, and he drove out the spirits with a word and healed all the sick. This was to fulfill what was spoken through the prophet Isaiah: 'He took up our infirmities and carried our diseases.'"

Acts 5:15,16: "As a result, people brought the sick into the streets and laid them on beds and mats so that at least Peter's shadow might fall on some of them as he passed by. Crowds gathered also from the towns around Jerusalem, bringing their sick and those tormented by evil spirits, and all of them were healed."

Acts 10:38: "How God anointed Jesus of Nazareth with the Holy Spirit and power, and how he went around doing good and healing all who were under the power of the devil, because God was with him."

1 Peter 2:24: "He himself bore our sins in his body on the tree, so that we might die to sins and live for righteousness; by his wounds you have been healed."

Another way to expose people to the Word of God is by giving them a book. I suggest *Healing the Sick* by T. L. Osborn, *Christ the Healer* by F. F. Bosworth, or a little booklet we have available entitled *Healing Scriptures*, which is an excerpt from the *Full-Life Study Bible*. The booklet is replete with Scriptures regarding healing.

For those who either don't want to read or cannot read because of their illness, you might want to provide a cassette tape player and cassette tape of healing Scriptures being read. Another helpful tool to provide is a set of Scripture posters the person can read while recovering. The posters need to be large enough to be read from across the room, and made with brightly colored pieces of paper and then laminated. Hang them on the walls of the hospital room in view of the patient to build faith.

V. Organize, Implement and Execute Licensing and Ordination Requirements and Procedures

Because ours is an independent church, our elders oversee the licensing and ordination of ministry candidates. Materials explaining licensing and ordination are available from the church office.

VI. Mediating Disputes Among the Brethren

Mediating disputes is one of the greatest provisions we have in our church administration. This provision leaves the pastors in a position to minister to the people involved in a dispute without becoming embroiled in it. And, it protects individual elders.

We use this system not only within our church, but also when believers from our church have major disputes with believers from other churches. In those instances, the case is heard by elders who are selected by our church and the other church. The senior pastors select elders who are not known to the people involved in the dispute so neither party is quite sure which elders are from their respective churches.

According to the Scriptures, believers in Christ are to settle disputes with other believers outside of secular courts of law. The following passages give us clear instructions about how we are to respond to those who disagree with us:

> Therefore, if you are offering your gift at the altar and there remember that your brother has something against you, leave your gift there in front of the altar. First go and be reconciled to your brother; then come and offer your gift.
>
> Settle matters quickly with your adversary who is taking you to court. Do it while you are still with him on the way, or he may hand you over to the judge, and the judge may hand you over to the officer, and you may be thrown into prison. I tell you the truth, you will not get out until you have paid the last penny (Matt. 5:23-26).

> You have heard that it was said, "Eye for eye, and tooth for tooth." But I tell you, Do not resist an evil person. If someone strikes you on the right cheek, turn to him the other also. And if someone wants to sue you and take your tunic, let him have your cloak as well. If someone forces you to go one mile, go with him two miles. Give to the one who asks you, and do not turn away from the one who wants to borrow from you (Matt. 5:38-42).

> If your brother sins against you, go and show him his fault, just between the two of you. If he listens to you, you have

won your brother over. But if he will not listen, take one or two others along, so that every matter may be established by the testimony of two or three witnesses. If he refuses to listen to them, tell it to the church; and if he refuses to listen even to the church, treat him as you would a pagan or a tax collector (Matt. 18:15-17).

If any of you has a dispute with another, dare he take it before the ungodly for judgment instead of before the saints? Do you not know that the saints will judge the world? And if you are to judge the world, are you not competent to judge trivial cases? Do you not know that we will judge angels? How much more the things of this life! Therefore, if you have disputes about such matters, appoint as judges even men of little account in the church! I say this to shame you. Is it possible that there is nobody among you wise enough to judge a dispute between believers? But instead, one brother goes to law against another—and this in front of unbelievers! The very fact that you have lawsuits among you means you have been completely defeated already. Why not rather be wronged? Why not rather be cheated? Instead, you yourselves cheat and do wrong, and you do this to your brothers (1 Cor. 6:1-8).

Prior to the mediation, all parties involved must be willing to voluntarily accept the decision of the elders as binding. The elders may invite the participation of other church members who are experts in the area of disagreement. And, when a dispute is being heard by the elders, those having the dispute must agree to allow the elders to confidentially speak with members of the pastoral staff who may have some insight.

If a dispute involves money, the number of elders required will be based on the following criteria:

Amount of Dispute

- $1 to $10,000: Three elders are to hear and decide this dispute or any disputes that don't involve monetary damages. Each party will select one elder, and the coordinating elder will select one elder. Two of the three elders must agree for a settlement.
- $10,001 to $100,000: Five elders are to hear and decide disputes of this size. Each party may select one elder and the coordinating elder is to select three. Three of the five elders must agree for a settlement.
- $100,001 or more: Seven elders are to hear a dispute of this size. Each party may select two elders and the coordinating elder will select three. Disputes of this magnitude require five of the seven to settle.

The individuals experiencing the dispute may ask people to send letters relating any pertinent information to the elders who are hearing the case. No limit is imposed on the number of letters that may be solicited or reviewed by the elders.

Each person involved in the dispute may bring two people to testify and answer questions during the mediation. One of the elders should open the meeting with prayer. Each side may take no more than one hour to present their case. Then the elders may question those present for as long as they feel is appropriate or necessary.

When the elders are satisfied with the information they have received, the elders should go to a private place to make a decision. Then they are to collectively communicate their decision to the parties involved at the same time in the same room. The opinions of individual elders are NOT to be expressed. Instead, all elders are only to express the final decision of the board.

After the decision has been communicated, the meeting should be closed in prayer, and the elders should remain for ministry if necessary.

VII. Counsel

Elders are to make themselves available as often as is reasonable to assist people within the church with biblical counsel or wisdom from their own experiences.

VIII. Confirm or Reject Pastoral Appointments to the Board of Trustees and the Board of Overseers

To maintain the highest level of accountability, we must have procedures that force us to check and balance one another. One of the ways we do this is by having our elders confirm or reject the people whom the senior pastor appoints as new members of both the board of trustees and the board of overseers.

The decision to either confirm or reject an appointment to these boards is done in accordance with Article Six, Section 4, Paragraph 1 and Article Eight, Paragraph 3 of our church Bylaws.

IX. Contact the Board of Overseers to Initiate Investigation and Potential Discipline of the Senior Pastor

Once again, accountability should always be a top priority, especially in the lives of those who are in positions of great responsibility and leadership. There should never be so much oversight that creativity and ability to lead with efficiency are hindered, but also, never so little that a leader is made unnecessarily vulnerable to the snares of the enemy.

In our system, the senior pastor may only be disciplined or removed for one of the following offenses:

1. Teaching that violates the creed of the church;
2. Misappropriation of funds;
3. Sexual misconduct.

If an elder is alerted to allegations against the senior pastor regarding any of these three offenses, the elder should meet with the pastor according to Matthew 18. If that meeting does not satisfy the elder, the elder and senior pastor may contact any member of the board of overseers to express their concerns. The overseers may then investigate the situation in compliance with Article Eight, Paragraph 3 of the church Bylaws.

X. Represent the Church to Other Churches

Most churches need representation from time to time at special events and with sister churches. In these situations, an elder may be the appropriate representative.

Section IV

Business That Strengthens the Life-Giving Church

13. Church Planting: First Things First
    With Joseph Thompson

14. Bylaws: Jethro's Request

Proper planting and organizing are vitally important to the protection of a life-giving church. Regardless of the role you have in ministry, understanding the subtitles of the next two chapters will assist your healthy participation in ministry for the rest of your life.

13

CHURCH PLANTING:
FIRST THINGS FIRST

WITH JOSEPH THOMPSON, ASSOCIATE PASTOR

IT [THE KINGDOM OF GOD] IS LIKE A MUSTARD
SEED, WHICH IS THE SMALLEST SEED YOU PLANT IN
THE GROUND. YET WHEN PLANTED, IT GROWS AND
BECOMES THE LARGEST OF ALL GARDEN PLANTS,
WITH SUCH BIG BRANCHES THAT THE BIRDS OF
THE AIR CAN PERCH IN ITS SHADE.

[*Mark 4:31,32*]

A Biblical Pattern

Just as children always reflect some of the attributes of their parents, so churches usually reflect the strengths and weaknesses of their founding. Here in Colorado Springs, we've seen many churches grow into powerful places of worship, while others have failed miserably. The reasons for the successes and failures are numerous, but the Bible does give us some hints to guide us in the planting of a healthy church. Exodus provides an amazingly helpful series of events that directly parallels the process necessary for planting a strong local church.

I. Recognize an Area of Need: Exodus 1

Exodus 1 portrays God's chosen people as needy and horribly oppressed. When planting a new church, we too must locate people with unusual needs. Chapter one of Exodus gives us an example for the placement of a church plant: a place where people are being harshly enslaved by darkness. Verse 11 says that Pharaoh "put slave masters over them to oppress them with forced labor." The Bible continues by reporting that the slave masters "made their lives bitter with hard labor in brick and mortar and with all kinds of work in the fields; in all their hard labor the Egyptians used them ruthlessly" (v. 14). This tyranny evolved into mass murder with Pharaoh ordering the slaughter of male babies born to Jewish mothers (see v. 22).

These verses canvass the ruthlessness of the powers of darkness enslaving people. Pharaoh, a type of Satan with his demonic influences, restrains God's people and, when necessary, murders any who might become a threat to his rule.

This scene, which demands God's liberating power, paints the backdrop for modern-day church plants; they should be strategically placed in oppressive, dark areas where the voice of God is only a whisper. The greater the darkness, the greater the need for light. For example, because of the darkness that oppresses people with such ruthlessness in so many cities, it might not be sound spiritual judgment to plant a church where an abundance of churches are already doing an effective work. Certainly, a need probably still exists in those areas, but the degree of need does not compare to those cities where there is less Christian influence.

This kind of thinking is standard in the world of missions. Currently, Dr. C. Peter Wagner of Fuller Seminary is coordinating prayer efforts specifically targeted at the world's darkest areas. Millions of intercessors from more than 120 countries are networking to focus their prayers toward the darkest areas of the earth.

At the same time, many outreach-evangelism groups are working on the heels of the prayer effort to follow up with tract and Bible distribution designed to promote church planting. Many believe that this generation can be the first to have the gospel available to every person on earth in his or her own language and culture. Because of the possibility, missiologists such as Dr. Wagner and others have wisely called all local churches to strategically focus their outreach efforts where they are most needed. As of this writing, 1,739 of the least evangelized people groups are being targeted with prayer and evangelism to bring at least a flicker of light to the darkest regions of the world.

Those efforts do not negate the fact that people in so-called reached areas have needs too. They do. All are needy. Some, however, are more needy than others. And God is calling us as believers to penetrate the darkness of the world with His light.

Sometimes, though, light tends to enjoy other light. It's more comfortable being one more light in a room with some light than going into a dark room to create only enough light to cast a shadow. We are called to be salt and light. Salt is better on food than in the shaker, and light shines brightest in darkness. Thus, when the spark that we carry is ignited by the wind of God's Spirit, we are neither burned out nor overcome by the foul breath of

———

WE ARE CALLED TO BE SALT AND LIGHT.

SALT IS BETTER ON FOOD THAN IN

THE SHAKER, AND LIGHT SHINES

BRIGHTEST IN DARKNESS.

———

demonic forces. Instead, we are fanned into life-giving flames that set the darkness ablaze.

So step number one should be to locate people who are in great need.

II. Appropriate Spiritual Authority: Exodus 2

Exodus 2 gives the account of when Moses "saw an Egyptian beating a Hebrew, one of his own people" (v. 11). In haste Moses killed the Egyptian, which embittered the Jewish people as well as the Egyptians against him. Because he was premature in his actions, Moses failed in providing any relief to his people. He didn't have the spiritual strength to confront Pharaoh, nor the spiritual authority to lead the Jewish people.

Moses was a good man, and he had been well trained. If being a man of God with fine training and good intentions had been the necessary combination for success, Moses would have achieved victory at this point. But Moses failed because he greatly lacked the spiritual authority needed to liberate others.

Being a well-trained, well-meaning Christian trying to do a church plant is not enough. We must be assured that God has appointed the timing, anointed the man and allocated a divine sense of spiritual strength for the task. When people show up and get excited about a new church plant, we can easily mistake their enthusiasm as a false signal for God's timing. And false starts do generate a degree of gratification, but they do not bring lasting results: Moses did kill the evil Egyptian, but that did not give him victory over Egypt, nor did it give him the right to lead the Jewish people to liberty. He won a little battle that, in fact, hurt rather than helped.

Many church plants start the same way, and usually lead to hurt feelings and discouraged leaders. "Unless the Lord builds the house [church plant or ministry], its builders labor in vain" (Ps. 127:1). Moses took the only sensible course of action available— he aborted the plan, got alone with God and allowed God to raise him up. If Moses had stayed, he would have been destroyed and God would have had to call another.

III. Receive a Divine Charge: Exodus 3
In Exodus 3 Moses encounters God through a burning bush. It is here that Moses receives a mandate and a blueprint from God for delivering the people of Israel out of their suffering. This is an essential step in successfully fulfilling God's call to plant churches. Only God's mandate can provide the spiritual strength and authority needed to win the war for the souls of men.

When God says, "Take off your sandals, for the place where you are standing is holy ground" (v. 5), He is demonstrating our need to have a divine, holy experience with Him. Part of that holy experience is God sharing His burdens with us. God explains in verses 7 and 8, "I have indeed seen the misery of my people in Egypt. I have heard them crying out because of their slave drivers, and I am concerned about their suffering. So I have come down to rescue them from the hand of the Egyptians" (emphasis added).

God is speaking to Moses about His concern for His people. He wants to partner with Moses in fulfilling His plan for Israel. But because Moses has learned the lesson so well from his hasty first mistake, he responds, "Who am I, that I should go to Pharaoh and bring the Israelites out of Egypt?" (v. 11). God likes that response. Moses' impulsive flesh and self-generated strength has now surrendered to the Master so God's plan can unfold. He starts giving Moses supernatural insight and strategy—fresh ideas.

I will never forget praying and fasting in a pup tent on the back of Pikes Peak. During those three days, God spoke deeply into my heart some things that burn in me to this day, 12 years later. He spoke to me about Praise Mountain, a prayer and fasting center that now exists in Florissant, Colorado. He spoke to me about New Life Church, which now exists in Colorado Springs. And He spoke to me about the World Prayer Center, which is currently under construction.

That was my burning bush experience, and because of it, the city looks different to me than it does to many. God spoke into my spirit what He thought of Colorado Springs and what He wanted the city to look like. He shared His plans. As the bush burns, it is never consumed. It just keeps speaking...forever.

To do a church plant without a divine charge creates a soulish church that lacks spiritual strength. But when the bush burns, it produces a humility that combines with boldness to create a foundation for action that is difficult to crack.

IV. Make Practical Preparations: Exodus 4

Even though God had spoken to Moses about His desire to liberate the Jewish people through his leadership, other practical issues still had to be settled. As those issues surface in Exodus 4, notice how they parallel those of the modern-day church plant. Moses needed:

A tangible sign from God (vv. 2-7). Moses' staff became a snake and then a staff again. God caused his hand to become leprous and restored it to normal. This same kind of supernatural confirmation is fundamental to pioneering a church plant. I don't believe the confirmation must always be as dramatic as that of Moses, but it must be enough to convince the church planter that there is enough empirical evidence to prove God has indeed spoken to him.

A friend (vv. 14-16). Note here that Moses does not need a board, a committee, government or structure to confront Pharaoh; he needs a friend. Moses feels inadequate, and his feelings frustrate and anger God. Nonetheless, God allows Moses' brother and friend, Aaron, to stand beside him to give strength and confidence. We learn later that Aaron alone is not strong, and we see here that Moses alone is not strong, but *together*, they can fulfill God's calling. In the same way, the success of a life-giving church plant will require the strength of loyal, sacrificial friendship. Genuine friendships empower people.

Submission to God's delegated authorities (v. 18). Even after this dramatic experience with God, Moses asked Jethro, his father-in-law for whom he was working, to give him permission to return to Egypt. God commands us to pray for all who are in authority over us so "we may live peaceful and quiet lives in all godliness and holiness" (1 Tim. 2:2). If we fail to pray for those in authority over us and fail to receive their blessing, the result can be unnecessary vulnerability. But Moses asked permission from his authority to do what God had commanded him to do, and God granted Moses' request through Jethro. This was, in effect, additional confirmation.

After my burning bush experience on the back side of Pikes Peak, I went to Roy Stockstill, my senior pastor for whom I was working at the time, and asked permission to move to Colorado Springs so I could fulfill my calling. He then flew from Baton Rouge, Louisiana, to Colorado Springs to meet with pastors and observe the city. When he returned, he told me that he could indeed see why God was calling me and he released me to go.

Obedience (vv. 24-26). Moses' wife, Zipporah, rescued Moses from the consequences of disobedience to God. When God called me to Colorado Springs, I was watching a baseball game as the Lord unexpectedly spoke into my spirit: *If you'll obey me, your effectiveness in Colorado Springs will be like this.* Immediately, the team I was watching started doing everything perfectly. It looked as though a professional team were playing against elementary school students. Then God said, *If you disobey me, you'll still be somewhat effective because of my grace, but your life will be like this.* Remarkably, the same team lost all ability. They couldn't hit, throw, catch or even communicate clearly. The game became a miserable, horrible experience for them. I got the picture. Obedience is a must.

Initial positive reception by the core of friends who shared his vision (vv. 29-31). Moses and Aaron met with the elders of Israel to share the vision, and God confirmed His plan to use Moses by performing the signs before them. The elders, therefore, believed that Moses was sent to them in answer to their prayers and worshiped God for his provision. Unity was established. We see here that, in order to do a church plant, a sense of unity, focus and purpose must be established among those who help to plant the church.

As soon as the practical preparation was complete, Moses, with Aaron at his side, was ready to confront Pharaoh.

V. Boldly Confront Demonic Strongholds: Exodus 5—11

Moses leads through influence, not corporate power. He gains his strength directly from the Lord and his relationships with his friends, not a formal committee. Notice, however, that when Moses is confronting the false gods of Egypt and demanding that they release the Jewish people in chapters 5 through 11, he does not call for a board meeting or a consultation to determine *what*

———

FRIENDSHIPS ARE AN IMPENETRABLE FORCE

BECAUSE OF THE FLEXIBILITY AND POWER

OF AN UNSPOKEN COVENANT.

———

God may be saying. Instead, Moses forcefully confronts the demonic strongholds that are empowering the Egyptians. That demonic hold on Israel is ultimately broken and then, with the Passover, comes the type of liberation through Christ.

These chapters on confrontation provide types of engaging prayer for us. Prayer is both communion and confrontation. Chapters 5-11 show the strength appropriated through Moses' communion with God for *confrontation* with darkness.

The confrontation begins when God instructs Moses to have Aaron throw down his staff before Pharaoh. The fact that Aaron is to throw down the staff, not Moses, is a testimony to the necessity for friends in the midst of battles.

When we were beginning New Life Church, a core of us worked together as friends. The relationships that formed because of our common purpose were much more important than any corporate positions, job descriptions or salaries. The innocence of the early days is very important as everyone works together, eats together, prays together and ministers together. No one worries about who should do what because of the friendships.

Without this understanding about relational ties, the spiritual battle required for the birthing of a local church in a needy area may be substituted with a corporate structure. When that happens, the forces of darkness easily infiltrate that birthing church and either kill it or at least control it, rendering it powerless.

Friendships are an impenetrable force because of the flexibility and power of an unspoken covenant. We see this type of empowering friendship with Moses and Aaron; David and Jonathan; Jesus and John; and Paul with his friends in Philippi. The list could go on and on, but the vital power of friendships must not be underestimated if we are to win the spiritual battles that will confront us as we begin a church plant.

The most important friendship of all, of course, is our relationship with Jesus Christ. He is the friend "who sticks closer than a brother" (Prov. 18:24), and it is the strength and connectedness we have with Him through a healthy, ongoing prayer life that will ultimately conquer our enemies.

Systematically, the Lord sent 10 different plagues to demonstrate that the God of Israel is more powerful than any of the gods of Egypt. In Colorado Springs a religious god of control had enslaved many churches. We had to confront it. We have also had to deal with other gods (evil spirits) in our area. Every community has demonic strategies that will attempt to enslave people. If that were not so, there would be no need for church plants.

These Egyptian gods were dealt with one at a time through the plagues that God sent. Sometimes demonic forces would respond to God's plagues by demonstrating their powers. Other times the demonic forces chose to hide or leave. That same pattern is consistent in any strong church plant. Threatened demonic powers may resist, not exist or simply surrender.

When the Nile turned to blood, the impotence of the water deity Iris was exposed. God sent a multitude of frogs and then killed them to demonstrate victory over Ptha and Heka, the Egyptian gods that glorified the supremacy of human life. Leb, the earth god, was embarrassed when God sent lice (gnats). The plague of flies was a blow against Khepara, the beetle god, god of the insects. The next plague was a plague of *murrain* (a general term implying a plague upon domestic animals) and was aimed at Apis (or Seraphis), the sacred cattle god at Memphis.

The plague of boils kept people from worshiping Neit, the Egyptian goddess, queen of heaven. Iris, the water god, and Osiris, the fire god, were proven inept when God sent the hail. And the locusts proved God's superiority over Shu, the god of the air. The final blow came when God demonstrated His sovereignty over Ra (or Atun Re), the sun god, the supreme god of Egypt, represented by Pharaoh himself. God sent darkness to the earth and brought death upon the firstborn of all Egyptians, including the son of Pharaoh.

Only after this awesome display of spiritual might did Pharaoh surrender and let God's people go. Similarly, the true effectiveness of church planting (delivering people from bondage to sin and death) is only realized after major confrontations with the forces of darkness have resulted in a supernatural display of God's might.

VI. Publicly Emphasize Jesus' Victory—Celebrate!
Exodus 12—17

Confrontation with the demonic will always yield good fruit, tangible evidence. The first Passover demonstrates for us the ministry of Christ's sacrifice, which opens the door for the liberation of the people from Satan's grasp. Moses leads the people out of Egypt and when they reach the Red Sea, the Lord causes it to supernaturally part, allowing the Israelites to cross over to the other side. This crossing through the Red Sea symbolizes a rebirth of the people of Israel—a metaphor for conversion growth in the New Testament Church.

In chapter 15 we see demonstrative praise and celebration— happy people. Victory and deliverance from oppression are celebrated as bitter water turns sweet, healing is promised and received, and springs and palm trees appear—all pictures of the celebration and the innocence that should engulf people in every church as they rejoice over their newfound freedom in Christ.

Chapters 16 and 17 give us a type of the New Testament Church complete with signs and wonders. God miraculously provides food in the form of manna from heaven and water from the rock to satisfy thirst. Both the manna and the rock point to Christ, and the water refers to the Holy Spirit.

Spiritual growth within the Body of Christ is where the strength of established friendships becomes even more apparent. We see Moses observing the Israelites in battle with the Amalekites from his vantage point on top of a hill. As long as his arms are raised to the heavens, Israel is victorious. As soon as Moses begins to tire and his arms start to drop, Amalek begins to win. Enter Aaron and Hur. They place a large rock under Moses so he is able to sit down. Then they hold up his arms, one on either side, to provide strength. Israel is victorious.

Joshua is fighting on the battlefield for Moses. Aaron and Hur hold Moses' hands up when he grows weary. Friendship increases the strength and integrity of the early victories in any church plant. Once the early battles have been won, the resulting growth is so overwhelming that soon a fully functioning church government needs to be in place. Thus, Moses is overwhelmed by his ministry load and Jethro recommends the establishment of a formal government.

VII. Now, Establish a Functional Church Government: Exodus 18

Now that the church has begun to experience numerical and spiritual growth, a system of governance should be put in place to serve the needs of the larger Body. Exodus 18 paints a clear picture of this process.

Moses is spending all of his time adjudicating disputes among the people when his father-in-law suggests that there is a better way to minister to their needs:

> Listen now to me and I will give you some advice, and may God be with you. You must be the people's representative before God and bring their disputes to him. Teach them the decrees and laws, and show them the way to live and the duties they are to perform. But select capable men from all the people—men who fear God, trustworthy men who hate dishonest gain—and appoint them as officials over thousands, hundreds, fifties and tens. Have them serve as judges for the people at all times, but have them bring every difficult case to you; the simple cases they can decide themselves. That will make your load lighter, *because they will share it with you.* If you do this and God so commands, you will be able to stand the strain, and all these people will go home satisfied (vv. 19-23, italics added).

This is a perfect illustration of some of the attendant problems with numerical growth. There comes a time when the weight of ministry needs to be shared simply because it is too overwhelming for one person. Under these circumstances the formation of a church government or corporation becomes essential for effective ministry to the Body.

The problem is further reiterated by Jethro's statement in verses 17 and 18:

What you are doing is not good. You and these people
who come to you will only wear yourselves out. The work
is too heavy for you; you cannot handle it alone.

When we started New Life Church, we had a basic church-
government system for processing funds and purchasing a few
small items, but the church didn't really function through the
church-government system in those early stages. Instead, the
governing process was similar to what Moses went through.

God called me for a specific task and my friends helped to
empower me to take risks. I was not rebellious. I was submissive
just as Moses was, but I was also decisive and directional. It was
not the time yet for boards and committees because I knew that,
even though others were called to join with me, they had not
heard what I had heard, nor seen what I had seen, nor were they
responsible for what God had told me to do. We did pray together, and many times in the midst of engaging prayer, we would
talk about what the Lord was doing. What little government we
had at that stage was not to make decisions, but to enable vision.
We only had enough government to serve, not to lead.

As in the case of Moses, in every successful church plant there
eventually comes a time to delegate areas of responsibility to
people who have proven themselves to be mature and faithful. At
that stage a defined corporate and spiritual structure must be set
in place to serve the Body.

Furthermore, after working through the steps of church planting right up to establishing a church government, a need arises to
provide a written law or statutes for the people. This process of
"receiving" the law is outlined in Exodus 19 and 20.

Moses meets with God on Mount Sinai and is given the Ten
Commandments as a guide for the people. The "Sinai experience"
only becomes relevant at the time a corporate structure is being
instituted. This enables the house vision to be clearly articulated
with defined roles and parameters established for every individual.

Exodus describes the step-by-step procedures we must go through to plant a church. If we can keep from bogging down in unnecessary complexity and unproductive structures, the life-giving flow that birthed the church will continue on into its maturity. Don't organize the corporate structure too soon. Instead, let life attract so many people that organization demands formation because of the volume of ministry required.

14

Bylaws:
Jethro's Request

THERE IS A TIME FOR EVERYTHING, AND A SEASON
FOR EVERY ACTIVITY UNDER HEAVEN.

[*Ecclesiastes 3:1*]

PEACE, PEACE, WONDERFUL PEACE

This final chapter is where the rubber meets the road. As I said earlier, staying in the tree of life is possible within any church structure, but some structures make ministry easy, while others unnecessarily complicate it.

This chapter is a set of recommended Bylaws with footnotes that explain the reasoning for the Bylaws. Some of these ideas you will like; others you will not. That's fine. Mark the ones you like and, if you decide to adopt them, consult an attorney to adapt the correct wording for the laws within your state. Take what you like and leave the rest. I would suggest, though, that spiritual freedom could be short-lived without structural freedom. These simple Bylaws give people the freedom to minister without providing a license to sin. Good combination.

Bylaws are the rules that govern an organization. I've seen some organizations that overemphasize their Bylaws and strangle the life out of everyone, and others that don't have any Bylaws; therefore, they find themselves in trouble when the unexpected happens. The Bylaws that follow are simple but thorough. I think you'll actually enjoy them. I know they can save you great heartache and provide the protection needed for effective ministry. So get a cup of coffee, a pen in hand to make some notes and sit back to enjoy them. Smile.

ARTICLE ONE

Offices

The principal office of [church name], hereinafter referred to as the Corporation, shall be located at the address set forth in the Articles of Incorporation. The Corporation may have such other offices, either within or without the State of Incorporation, as the board of trustees may determine.[1]

---

1. If you are leasing, it is important that the principal office of the Corporation be an address that is consistent. Most states allow a residential address to be used if the meeting location is transitional. However, if you have a permanent church location, that is the address to use.

ARTICLE TWO

Membership

Members shall be all people who contribute financially to the Corporation (church). Membership is granted and recognized with voting powers when a person has attended the church long enough to receive an annual contributions statement. A contribution statement is the certificate of membership. Should one year pass without a record of contribution, membership is automatically terminated. Members' voting rights are described in Article Nine, Paragraph 5, relating to nominations for the board of elders and Article Five, relating to the selection of a new senior pastor. Members shall have no other voting rights.[2]

---

2. This bylaw is the balance between those who strongly emphasize church membership and those who have no formal membership at all.
    I believe people need to know what determines their membership in their local church, and I think the pastor needs to know who is a member and who is not. But membership should be structured so the leadership team is 100 percent consumed with drawing people into a relationship with the Lord, not the church. Once people establish a relationship with the Lord, their natural responses signal that they have

become members of the Church.

I don't think it's wise to have too many hoops to jump through or barriers to hurdle to become a member. Actually, I've observed that when people start referring to the church in the first person, "my church" or "our church" it means that their hearts have been added to the church Body. Once again, strive for balance. People need to be strongly committed to the local church without a hyper sense of obligation. That is what this article allows.

ARTICLE THREE

Statement of Faith[3]

Holy Bible: The Holy Bible, and only the Bible, is the authoritative Word of God. It alone is the final authority for determining all doctrinal truths. In its original writing, the Bible is inspired, infallible and inerrant (see Prov. 30:5; Rom. 16:25,26; 2 Tim. 3:16; 2 Pet. 1:20,21).

Trinity: There is one God, eternally existent in three persons: Father, Son (Jesus) and Holy Spirit. These three are coequal and coeternal (see Gen. 1:26; Isa. 9:6; Matt. 3:16,17; 28:19; Luke 1:35; Heb. 3:7-11; 1 John 5:7).

Jesus Christ: Jesus Christ is God the Son, the second person of the Trinity. On earth, Jesus was 100 percent God and 100 percent man. He is the only man *ever* to have lived a sinless life. He was born of a virgin, lived a sinless life, performed miracles, died on the Cross for humankind and, thus, atoned for our sins through the shedding of His blood. He rose from the dead on the third day according to the Scriptures, ascended to the right hand of the Father, and will return again in power and glory (see Isa. 9:6; John 1:1,14; 20:28; Phil. 2:5,6; 1 Tim. 2:5; 3:16).

Virgin Birth: Jesus Christ was conceived by God the Father, through the Holy Spirit (the third person of the Trinity) in the virgin Mary's womb; therefore, He is the Son of God (see Isa. 7:14; Matt. 1:18,23-25; Luke 1:27-35).

Redemption: Humanity was created good and upright, but by voluntary transgression, it fell. Humanity's only hope for redemption is in Jesus Christ, the Son of God (see Gen. 1:26-31; 3:1-7; Rom. 5:12-21).

Regeneration: For anyone to know God, regeneration by the Holy Spirit is absolutely essential (see John 6:44,65).

Salvation: We are saved by grace through faith in Jesus Christ: His death, burial and resurrection. Salvation is a gift from God, not a result of our good works or of any human effort (see Rom. 10:9,10; Acts 16:31; Gal. 2:16; 3:8; Eph. 2:8,9; Titus 3:5; Heb. 9:22).

Repentance: Repentance is the commitment to turn away from sin in every area of our lives and to follow Christ, which allows us to receive His redemption and to be regenerated by the Holy Spirit. Thus, through repentance we receive forgiveness of sins and appropriate salvation (see Acts 2:21; 3:19; 1 John 1:9).

Sanctification: Sanctification is the ongoing process of yielding to God's Word and His Spirit in order to complete the development of Christ's character in us. It is through the present ministry of the Holy Spirit and the Word of God that the Christian is enabled to live a godly life (see Rom. 8:29; 12:1,2; 2 Cor. 3:18; 6:14-18; 1 Thess. 4:3; 5:23; 2 Thess. 2:1-3; Heb. 2:11).

Jesus' Blood: The blood Jesus Christ shed on the cross of Calvary was sinless and is 100 percent sufficient to cleanse humankind from all sin. Jesus allowed Himself to be punished for both our sinfulness and our sins, enabling all those who believe to be free from the penalty of sin, which is death (see John 1:29; Rom. 3:10-12,23; 5:9; Col. 1:20; 1 John 1:7; Rev. 1:5; 5:9).

Jesus Christ Indwells All Believers: Christians are people who have invited the Lord Jesus Christ to come and live inside them by His Holy Spirit. They relinquish the authority of their lives over to Him, thus making Jesus the Lord of their lives as well as Savior. They put their trust in what Jesus accomplished for them when He died, was buried and rose again from the dead (see John 1:12; 14:17,23; 15:4; Rom. 8:11; Rev. 3:20).

Baptism in the Holy Spirit: Given at Pentecost, the baptism in the Holy Spirit is the promise of the Father. It was sent by Jesus after His Ascension to empower the Church to preach the gospel throughout the whole earth (see Joel 2:28,29; Matt. 3:11; Mark 16:17; Acts 1:5; 2:1-4,17,38,39; 8:14-17; 10:38,44-47; 11:15-17; 19:1-6).

The Gifts of the Holy Spirit: The Holy Spirit is manifested through a variety of spiritual gifts to build and sanctify the Church, demonstrate the validity of the Resurrection and confirm the power of the gospel. The lists of these gifts in the Bible are not necessarily exhaustive, and the gifts may occur in various combinations. All believers are commanded to earnestly desire the manifestation of the gifts in their lives. These gifts always operate in harmony with the Scriptures and should never be used in violation of biblical parameters (see Rom. 1:11; 12:4-8; 1 Cor. 12:1-31; 14:1-40; Eph. 4:16; 1 Tim. 4:14; 2 Tim. 1:5-16; Heb. 2:4; 1 Pet. 4:10).

The Church: The Church is the Body of Christ, the habitation of God through the Spirit, with divine appointments for the fulfillment of Jesus' Great Commission. Every person born of the Spirit is an integral part of the Church as a member of the Body of believers. There is a spiritual unity of all believers in our Lord Jesus Christ (see John 17:11,20-23; Eph. 1:22; 2:19-22; Heb. 12:23).

Two Sacraments:

Water Baptism: Following faith in the Lord Jesus Christ, the new convert is commanded by the Word of God to be baptized in water in the name of the Father, and of the Son, and of the Holy Spirit (see Matt. 28:19; Acts 2:38).[4]

The Lord's Supper: A unique time of communion in the presence of God when the elements of bread and grape juice (the body and blood of the Lord Jesus Christ) are taken in remembrance of Jesus' sacrifice on the cross (see Matt. 26:26-29; Mark 16:16; Acts 8:12,36-38; 10:47,48; 1 Cor. 10:16; 11:23-26).

Healing of the Sick: Healing of the sick is illustrated in the life and ministry of Jesus, and included in Jesus' commission to His disciples. Healing of the sick is given as a sign that is to follow believers. It is also a part of Jesus' work on the cross and one of the gifts of the Spirit (see Ps. 103:2,3; Isa. 53:5; Matt. 8:16,17; Mark 16:17,18; Acts 8:6,7; Rom. 11:29; 1 Cor. 12:9,28; Jas. 5:14-16).

God's Will for Provision: The Father's will is that believers become whole, healthy and successful in all areas of life. But because of the Fall, many may not receive the full benefits of God's will while on earth. That fact, though, should never prevent all believers from seeking the full benefits of Christ's provision in order to serve others.

- Spiritual (see John 3:3-11; Rom. 10:9,10; 2 Cor. 5:17-21).
- Mental and emotional (see Isa. 26:3; Rom. 12:2; Phil. 4:7,8; 2 Tim. 1:7; 2:11).
- Physical (see Isa. 53:4,5; Matt. 8:17; 1 Pet. 2:24).
- Financial (see Deut. 28:1-14; Josh. 1:8; Ps. 34:10; 84:11; Mal. 3:10,11; Luke 6:38; 2 Cor. 9:6-10; Phil. 4:19).

Resurrection: Jesus Christ was physically resurrected from the dead in a glorified body three days after His death on the cross. As a result, both the saved and the lost will be resurrected—they that are saved to the resurrection of life, and they that are lost to the resurrection of eternal damnation (see Luke 24:16,36,39; John 2:19-21; 20:26-28; 21:4; Acts 24:15; 1 Cor. 15:42,44; Phil. 1:21-23; 3:21).

Heaven: Heaven is the eternal dwelling place for all believers in the gospel of Jesus Christ (see Matt. 5:3,12,20; 6:20; 19:21; 25:34; John 17:24; 2 Cor. 5:1; Heb. 11:16; 1 Pet. 1:4).

Hell: After living one life on earth, the unbelievers will be judged by God and sent to hell where they will be eternally tormented with the devil and the fallen angels (see Matt. 25:41; Mark 9:43-48; Heb. 9:27; Rev. 14:9-11; 20:12-15; 21:8).

Second Coming: Jesus Christ will physically and visibly return to earth for the second time to establish His kingdom. This will occur at a date undisclosed by the Scriptures (see Matt. 24:30; 26:63,64; Acts 1:9-11; 1 Thess. 4:15-17; 2 Thess. 1:7,8; Rev. 1:7).

3. The statement of faith should say exactly what you want the church to believe throughout the generations. Your statement of faith is the way to protect the church, because no senior pastor can ever serve the church who does not believe and teach the creed of the church. To violate the creed is reason for dismissal.

4. We have chosen not to fight over our baptism formula. Matthew 28:19 says, "Therefore go and make disciples of all nations, baptizing them in the name of the Father and of the Son and of the Holy Spirit." Acts 2:38 says, "Peter replied, 'Repent, and let every one of you be baptized in the name of Jesus Christ for the remission of sins; and you shall receive the gift of the Holy Spirit.'"

So when we baptize in water, we say, "I baptize you in the name of the Father, and of the Son, and of the Holy Spirit, in the name of Jesus Christ." That way we cover all of the scriptural instructions regarding water baptism.

ARTICLE FOUR

Government

[Church name] is governed by the congregation, the trustees of the Corporation, the office of the senior pastor and the overseers. The congregation determines the spiritual tone, strength and direction of the church by wisely selecting the senior pastor. The trustees are to serve the church by setting policy in the management of the church Corporation and making the major financial decisions for the church. The senior pastor's office is responsible for overseeing the day-to-day ministry of the church, and the board of overseers is to protect the church through counsel, prayer and, if required, the discipline of the senior pastor.[5]

5. This article formally introduces the balanced combination of the four primary methods of church government. All churches use these basic systems to one degree or another, but we use each of these in their most positive function, resulting in an excellent separation of power and clearly defined roles.

ARTICLE FIVE

Congregation

Section 1. General Authority to Select a New Senior Pastor[6]
Should the church need a new senior pastor, two methods are
provided for the congregational selection of a new senior pastor.
One method involves the participation of the departing pastor;
the other method does not. The founding pastor of the church
need not be officially confirmed by the congregation; therefore,
he is exempted from Article Five.

Section 2. Congregational Process with the Participation of the
Departing Pastor[7]

(Paragraph 1) Departing Pastor Participates in
Replacement
If the senior pastor is in good standing with the church
and is removing himself because of retirement or relo-
cation, the following is the selection process:

(Paragraph 2) Congregational Vote
The senior pastor may choose up to two candidates.
The first candidate is to speak in three or more of the
primary church services. Then the senior pastor is to
formally recommend this candidate during a Monday
night meeting of the membership. The meeting is to
be announced in the primary services of the church
and held eight days later on a Monday night. Any
meeting of the membership for pastoral selection
requires that members bring their contribution
records from the previous year and display them at
the door in order to verify membership. At that meeting, the departing senior pastor and the candidate
must leave. Then the secretary/treasurer is to conduct
a secret ballot vote and, with a minimum two-thirds
(2/3) vote, the candidate shall be accepted. If that can-

didate fails, the second candidate chosen by the senior pastor is afforded the same opportunity as the
first. If the second ballot fails, the process outlined in
Section 3 shall be followed.

Section 3. Congregational Process Without Departing Pastor's
Participation[8]

(Paragraph 1) Departing Pastor Unavailable
If the senior pastor is removed by the overseers, is
deceased, or cannot or will not participate in the
selection process of the new senior pastor for any
reason, the following shall be the process for selecting a new senior pastor:

(Paragraph 2) Meeting of the Membership
The secretary/treasurer or another person appointed by
the board of trustees is to immediately call a meeting
of the membership by making an announcement during the primary service(s). The meeting is to be held in
the church building on a Monday night, eight days later.
At the meeting of the membership, a Pastoral Selection
Committee of nine people will be elected by the membership—to include three men and three women from
the general membership and the three most senior full-
time pastoral staff members. If there are not three full-
time pastoral staff members, the membership may elect
people who are familiar with the day-to-day work of
the church. The committee itself is to vote and select a
chairperson and cochairperson.

(Paragraph 3) Formation of Pastoral Selection
    Committee
The duty of the Pastoral Selection Committee is to

provide an interim pastor or guest speakers to conduct church services. However, neither an interim pastor nor a replacement speaker shall have the corporate powers of the president.

(Paragraph 4) Congregational Vote
The committee is to recommend a new senior pastor as soon as an acceptable candidate is available. That person must be a licensed or ordained minister of the gospel. He must be approved by three of the five members on the board of overseers before being presented to the church. Once the committee recommends a senior pastoral candidate, that person may speak to the church in every service for three weeks or in at least three of the primary church services. Afterward, a meeting of the membership shall be publicly called on a Monday night, chaired by the secretary/treasurer or by a member of the board of trustees selected by that board. At that meeting church members shall vote by secret ballot to either accept or reject the pastoral candidate. Trustees and their spouses are to count the ballots. A minimum two-thirds (2/3) vote of those attending the meeting is required to elect the next senior pastor. When a two-thirds (2/3) majority in favor of the candidate does not occur, the Pastoral Selection Committee shall seek another candidate.

(Paragraph 5) Staff Administration During Transition
During the selection process, members of the church staff are to continue in their positions. Should staff or financial problems arise, the secretary/treasurer has authority to alter the roles of staff members, including dismissal if necessary in the judgment of

the secretary/treasurer. When the new senior pastor is in place, he has full authority to select his own staff, replacing existing staff members, if he should choose, according to the severance agreements (Article Seven, Section 2, Paragraph 5).[9]

6. This section allows congregational government in the selection of a new senior pastor. This process is vitally important in light of the great freedoms the senior pastor is given under these Bylaws. Those freedoms are necessary for effective and powerful leadership, which places a great deal of responsibility on the people who select him. Remember, once the senior pastor is selected, he will direct the spiritual countenance of the entire church for potentially many, many years.

   Don't rush the process. The easiest way to fire someone is to never hire him. And, with this form of government, the person cannot be fired unless a serious offense has been committed. And even then, the overseers are the only people who can dismiss him. So be wise.

   Because of its importance, this selection process has two parts explained in Sections 2 and 3.

7. This process is to be used if the current senior pastor is leaving in good standing. That means he is trusted and respected, and therefore should be fully involved in the appointment of the person who will succeed him.

8. This process is more cumbersome than the first because it provides for the situation where the most recent senior pastor is not present due to death, dismissal or a resignation when the pastor chooses not to participate. The goal is to select God's man as the senior pastor. Don't become sidetracked by the process. Always remember the goal.

9. It is proper and right for employees hired by the previous senior pastor to make themselves available for resignation anytime within a two-year window of the new senior pastor's placement. The new senior pastor should have the freedom to replace past employees at will during his first two years. This courtesy by the employees is a great contribution to the continued health of the church.

ARTICLE SIX

Trustees of the Corporation
Section 1. General Powers[10]
The major financial affairs of the Corporation shall be managed by

the board of trustees, hereinafter referred to as the trustees, whose members shall have a fiduciary obligation to the Corporation.
Section 2. Functions[11]

(Paragraph 1) Provide Facilities
The trustees vote in accordance with these Bylaws in order to conduct the major business decisions of the Corporation. The trustees oversee the provision of the physical facilities needed by the church Body. They also coordinate any construction projects that require a loan.

(Paragraph 2) Exclusive Authority
The trustees are the only body within the Corporation or church Body with the authority to (1) buy and sell real estate, (2) borrow money and/or (3) secure real estate leases.

(Paragraph 3) Counsel[12]
The trustees are to provide counsel to the senior pastor regarding the major financial affairs of the church.

(Paragraph 4) Staff Loans
Any employee of the church requesting financial assistance from the church in the form of a loan must first obtain permission from the senior pastor to apply for the loan. The trustees shall then review the application. All terms and conditions of the loan must be approved by a majority (four or more) of the trustees.

No loans shall be made to any officer or trustee of the Corporation.

Section 3. Financial Guidelines[13]

(Paragraph 1) Moneys Available to Trustees
In order to provide for the physical needs of the church, the trustees have available to them 100 percent of all unrestricted moneys accumulated in any type of savings account (including stocks, bonds, CDs, mutual funds, etc.) and all assets in land and property. In addition, the trustees may direct any expenditures up to 35 percent of the unrestricted income of the church from tithes, offerings, interest and investments. (Current undesignated income is 90 percent of the undesignated income of the previous year.) From the 35 percent of church income at the trustees' disposal, payment must be made on all debts and real estate leases of the Corporation.

(Paragraph 2) Debt Restrictions[14]
Before the trustees may authorize the church to borrow money or incur a lease obligation, the following conditions must be met:

1. Minimum 25 percent down. Should the trustees choose to borrow money to facilitate the growth and/or work of the church, they must first accumulate 25 percent of the total price for the project as a down payment. Two variables apply when determining whether sufficient funds have been accumulated. One, amounts previously expended on the project to be financed from the proceeds of such indebtedness will be deemed accumulated. And two, amounts previously expended as principle reduction payments above minimum required payments on preexisting loans during the 12 months prior to incurring addi-

tional debt will be deemed accumulated and credited toward the 25 percent.

2. <u>Maximum 35 percent payment ceiling</u>. The combined totals of all monthly debt service and lease payments, following the incurring of the indebtedness or lease obligation under consideration, will not exceed 35 percent of the average monthly undesignated income. The percentage shall be based on, but not be limited to, tithes, offerings, investment income and unrestricted gifts of the church.

3. <u>Lease to purchase allowance</u>. If indebtedness is being secured to build a structure that will relieve the church of its need for a leased facility to be vacated when the new building is completed, then the current lease commitment need not be calculated into the 35 percent expenditure limitation for 18 months. Thus, the church is allowed 18 months for both construction and lease payments that combined, exceed the 35 percent limit, but only if compelling assurance is evidenced that by the end of the 18-month period reasonable relief can be expected from the burden of the lease payment.

4. <u>Income projections</u>. The church may *not* set budgets, meet conditions for borrowing or make any financial commitments based on upward projections of income.

5. <u>Audit requirements.</u> If the church wishes to borrow more than $250,000, the trustees must base their financial limitations on information provided by an audit of the previous year.

6. Church plant exception. If the church has less than
12 months financial history and wishes to borrow less
than $250,000, that decision may be based on the
most current 3 months of financial history provided
by the church treasurer. Even in this situation, the 25
percent down and 35 percent debt service ceilings
must be met.

(Paragraph 3) Annual Audit
If the income of the church exceeds $250,000 per year,
the trustees shall obtain an annual audit performed by
an independent public accounting firm in accordance
with Generally Accepted Auditing Standards (GAAS),
with financial statements prepared in accordance with
Generally Accepted Accounting Principles (GAAP).

(Paragraph 4) Audit Review Committee
The trustees shall appoint the secretary/treasurer and
two other members of the trustee board to serve as
an audit review committee. After reviewing the
annual audit, committee members are to report their
findings at a trustee meeting.

(Paragraph 5) Conflict of Interest
In order to avoid a conflict of interest, all the following criteria must be met to complete any business
transaction between a trustee and the Corporation:

1. The trustee with whom the transaction is being
considered is excluded from any discussions for
approving the transaction.

2. The trustees consider competitive bids or comparable
valuations.

3. The trustees act upon and demonstrate that the transaction is in the best interest of the Corporation.

4. The transaction must be fully disclosed in the end-of-year audited financial statements of the Corporation.

Section 4. Appointment, Number, Term and Qualifications[15]

(Paragraph 1) Number and Selection
The trustees shall be composed of seven members, who are appointed by the senior pastor and approved by the board of elders. Trustees may not be employees of the Corporation or staff members of the church, nor can they be related or married to employees or staff members. Any trustee appointed after [insert appropriate date] shall be approved by the board of elders (see Article Nine). The term of office for each trustee shall continue until such trustee resigns from office or from membership in the church, dies or is removed. All trustees must be selected from the membership of the church.

(Paragraph 2) Removal
The pastor may dismiss trustees without cause, but at a rate that does not exceed one dismissal every six months. The elders are not required to approve pastoral dismissals of trustees. In the event that the office of pastor is vacant, the secretary/treasurer may appoint or dismiss trustees subject to the same limitations that apply to appointments and dismissals by the senior pastor in accordance with this paragraph and Article Six, Section 4, Paragraph 1.

(Paragraph 3) Exclusive Role
Because the trustees are responsible for the major financial decisions of the church, they must resign their positions on the board if they ever become staff members or take any other paid position within the church. Volunteer work within the church is encouraged, but paid positions may constitute a conflict of interest.

Section 5. Meetings[16]

(Paragraph 1) Frequency of Meetings
A meeting of the trustees shall be held at least twice a year. The senior pastor, or any trustee may call a meeting at any time, under the condition that a majority (four or more) of the trustees attend the meeting.

(Paragraph 2) Leadership of Meetings
If at all possible, the senior pastor is to attend and lead each trustee meeting. If not possible, the secretary/treasurer shall lead the meeting. If neither the pastor nor the secretary/treasurer is able to lead the meeting, the trustees must choose a leader for that meeting and proceed in order, with an appointed member keeping minutes for the record. Any motions passed and recorded in a meeting without the pastor or the secretary/treasurer may not take effect until the following meeting with either the pastor or the secretary/treasurer present when the minutes of the previous meeting are approved.

(Paragraph 3) Location of Meetings
Any meeting of the trustees may be held at such place or places as shall from time to time be deter-

mined by the trustees or fixed by the senior pastor and designated in the notice of the meeting.

(Paragraph 4) Written Notice of Meetings
Whenever a written notice is required to be given to any trustee, these three rules apply: (1) Such notice may be given in writing by fax or by mail at such fax number or address as appears on the books of the Corporation and such notice shall be deemed to be given at the time the notice is faxed or mailed. (2) The person entitled to such notice may waive the notice by signing a written waiver before, at or after the time of the meeting. (3) The appearance of such person or persons at the meeting shall be equivalent to signing a written waiver of notice.

(Paragraph 5) Regular Meetings
The trustees may establish regular meetings. No notice shall be required for any regular meeting.

(Paragraph 6) Trustee Action Without Meeting
Any action that could be taken at a meeting of the trustees may be taken without a notice if at least four of the trustees participate with either the pastor or secretary/treasurer present. Such action shall be effective as of the date of the meeting.

(Paragraphs 7) Teleconferencing
At any meeting of the trustees, any person may participate in the meeting by telephone provided all members of the trustees present at the meeting or by telephone can hear and speak to each other. Participation by telephone shall be equivalent to attending the meeting in person.

(Paragraph 8) Quorum
A majority (four or more) of the trustees shall constitute a quorum for the transaction of business at any
meeting. The act of a majority of the trustees shall be
the act of the board of trustees. In the absence of a
quorum at any meeting, a meeting of the trustees
present may adjourn the meeting without further
notice until a quorum shall be established.

Section 6. Compensation
Trustees, as such, shall not receive any salaries for their services.

10. This section clarifies that the board has the fiduciary responsibility for the Corporation.
11. This section explains roles that only the board of trustees can fulfill. Most churches could have avoided problems over the exercise of authority if this section had been in their Bylaws. This section firmly establishes the Corporate board as the servant of the spiritual Body of believers, and will only allow the board to take action once the spiritual Body has demonstrated financial strength. This section is a great protection for the senior pastor and the church Body at large.
12. Counsel for the senior pastor can be interpreted as pressure. Therefore, the trustees are responsible for discussing with the senior pastor items helpful to his decision-making processes. I talk regularly with board members in stand-up meetings before or after a church service, discussing different issues. This does not require a board meeting format or setting. Because different members on the board have different areas of expertise, I casually talk with our trustees when I see them at the church to get input. This is always helpful.
13. This section provides the framework the trustees can use to serve the church. It is a provision to keep anyone from placing too much money in buildings and not enough in direct ministry toward people. All moneys saved, and up to 35 percent of the income of the church, can be used by the trustees, but the amount cannot exceed these limits. This limitation is a protection for the ministry aspects of the church. People love knowing that their tithes and offerings are going to ministry, not just buildings, and that even in times of expansion, no more than 35 percent of their tithes and offerings to the church go toward construction and debt service. This provision is a great motivator for the people in their giving. And it does allow the pastor to choose to

save as much as he would like toward a project. The limitation is only on indebtedness, not savings.

14. This section including its six subparagraphs keeps the church from incurring too much debt. It requires past performance before borrowing. Really, it keeps the church from making a financial mistake based on a dream, speculation or what people perceive as God's direction. These requirements do not unduly restrict, but provide a realistic constraint from overly aggressive financial commitments. With the 25 percent minimum down, 35 percent limit on payments, the congregation is secure and the business people will perceive the church as wise and conservative. This plan works well for all.

15. Some complain that in a beginning church, it is impossible to have seven people who could fulfill the role of a trustee board. If that is the case, you might not be ready to have a church structure. (Some rural communities would be one exception.) Maybe a Bible study format would be adequate with a club account at the bank. Then, when your group has grown to the point that seven people could fill trustee positions, incorporate and begin the actual process of establishing a working church structure.

Remember that this board is not an elder board or a deacon board, so these people do not have to meet the biblical requirements for spiritual leadership in the church. This is a business board. Choose people who have a steady, consistent walk with Christ, have long-lasting, positive relationships and are financially responsible. Select people who have proven themselves responsible in other, natural areas of life. If a person wants authority or says he/she would like to be a trustee, respectfully decline. Watch out for subtle forms of pseudo-submission to win your favor. Choose people who are genuine servants and love God. They will always be a blessing. Lastly, make sure they love you so they will utilize the Corporation to serve the Body of believers in a way that glorifies Christ.

Balance is achieved through the pastor's responsibility to appoint trustees. Should a pastor, however, want to change the board too quickly, he is limited in that he can only appoint and dismiss one trustee every six months. This stipulation protects everyone, and leaves proper balance of power in case of a difficulty. Provision is also made here should the pastor no longer be with the church. In that case, the overseers can appoint or dismiss trustees, keeping the church functional for a long interval without a pastor.

16. Don't have unnecessary meetings. If the church is building or moving, meet once a month. We meet on the second Sunday afternoon of every month at 4:00 P.M. when there is business. If not, we meet at the beginning of the year to review audit reports and in the fall for an update.

That's all that needs to be done unless money is being borrowed, land purchased or buildings being built. Keep it simple.

ARTICLE SEVEN

Senior Pastor of the Church/
President of the Corporation
Section 1. The Office of the Senior Pastor[17]

(Paragraph 1) The Dual Role
Because [church name] has two complementary branches-the spiritual Body of believers and the legal Corporation-it is the senior pastor who administratively bridges the gap between the two branches. This dual role can sometimes be awkward: The senior pastor is primarily responsible for the spiritual life of the church, therefore, he must be in a position corporately to ensure that financial strength is directed toward the ministries of his choice.

(Paragraph 2) Responsibilities of the Senior Pastor
It is the senior pastor's responsibility to:

- Provide biblical vision and direction for the congregation;
- Define and communicate the church's purpose;
- Oversee and coordinate the day-to-day ministry of the congregation and administration of the church;
- Appoint a board of overseers pursuant to Article Eight;
- Recognize and enlist apostolic, prophetic, evangelistic, pastoral and teaching ministries, along with elders, deacons and additional staff members as he deems biblical and necessary for the healthy spiritual development of the Body of believers;

- Select trustees pursuant to Article Six who will help oversee the business of the Corporation;
- Staff the church as he deems necessary to help administrate the affairs of the Corporation;
- Veto any nominations to the board of elders pursuant to Article Nine.

(Paragraph 3) The Pastor's Spiritual Leadership
The senior pastor may work with overseers, elders, deacons or anyone serving in the functions or offices as outlined in Ephesians 4:11-13 in whatever way he determines is biblical to serve the spiritual needs of the congregation. Additionally, the senior pastor may budget moneys, hire staff, develop projects, create cell groups, programs or other ministries according to his convictions and biblical understanding. He shall have the authority to appoint and approve any assistants necessary to properly carry on the work of the church.

(Paragraph 4) The Pastor's Responsibility for Services
Times, order of services and the leadership of services are to be determined by the senior pastor or by the spiritual church structure he establishes. No person shall be invited to speak, teach or minister at a service held in church-owned facilities, or in the name of the church, without the approval of the pastor or the appropriate member of the established church ministry team.

Section 2. The Office of the President[18]

(Paragraph 1) The President
The Corporation finds its leadership under the Lord

Jesus Christ and in its president. The senior pastor shall serve as the president and chief executive officer of the Corporation. If possible, he shall preside at all meetings of the board of trustees and shall see that all orders and resolutions of the board are put into effect. He shall execute in the name of the Corporation all deeds, bonds, mortgages, contracts and other documents authorized by the board of trustees. He shall be an ex-officio member of all standing committees, and shall have the general powers and duties of supervision and management usually vested in the office of the president of a corporation.

(Paragraph 2) The President's Role with Trustees
The president is the nonvoting chairman of the board of trustees. He calls meetings and determines the agenda in consultation with the trustees. The president shall make selections to the board of trustees from the church membership at a rate not to exceed one new appointment every six months in accordance with Article Six. The president may also dismiss trustee members, but at a rate that does not exceed one dismissal every six months in accordance with Article Six, Section 4, Paragraph 2.

(Paragraph 3) The President's Administrative Role[19]
The president is the senior administrator of the church. He is ultimately responsible for all day-to-day administrative decisions of the church.

(Paragraph 4) The President's Role with Staff[20]
The president hires, directs and dismisses staff. As the senior pastor, his call is confirmed to the church

through the congregation, and those hired by him are to assist him in fulfilling this calling.

(Paragraph 5) The President's Role in Establishing Salaries

The president determines all salaries and writes pay scales for full-time salaried employees. Pay scales shall be explained to new full-time salaried employees. Changes in pay scales will be given in writing to the affected employees. If a severance-pay agreement is established, that too must be given to the employee in writing. In addition, all part-time salaries and hourly wages are variable and are to be determined between the president and the employee.

(Paragraph 6) The President's Salary Exceptions[21]

The salary of the president is to be on the same pay scale consistent with the pay scale established for the other members of the pastoral team with the following two exceptions:

1. Housing: The president (senior pastor) may live in a parsonage owned and maintained by the Corporation. The board of trustees shall choose the parsonage.

2. Transportation: The senior pastor shall be provided with two automobiles, which will be maintained by the Corporation. The trustees shall determine the cost of the automobiles. The Corporation shall then purchase or lease the vehicle of the pastor's choice within the budget allowed. Each automobile is to be kept for six years. During his first three years of service at the church, only one automobile shall be pro-

vided; then, at the beginning of the fourth year, the second shall be purchased or leased. Henceforth, a new vehicle is to be purchased or leased every three years. If the president chooses to replace a vehicle before six years expires, the value remaining in the previous vehicle is the maximum that may be spent unless the president contributes personal funds toward the purchase of the replacement vehicle. No additional funds may be added by the Corporation for the purchase of a vehicle out of sequence.

(Paragraph 7) Optional Benefits
After the senior pastor has served for a minimum of 10 consecutive years, the trustees may provide additional benefits unique to the senior pastoral position. They may, for example, choose to provide an additional retirement benefit to compensate for the senior pastor's inability to build equity in a home while living in a church-owned parsonage. The trustees may also choose to reduce the amount of time the senior pastor is required to keep a vehicle before replacing it. These benefits and others like them must be initiated by the trustees rather than the senior pastor because these benefits are optional and not required. They are purely an attempt to reward many years of faithful service.

(Paragraph 8) Budget[22]
After the church is one year old, an annual budget must be prepared. The budget is to be based on 90 percent of the previous year's undesignated income. The president is to write the budget for 65 percent of the 90 percent in order to finance the basic ministry needs of the church (salaries, taxes, bills, missions,

benevolence, department financial allocations, etc.). He is free to reflect his values and wisdom in his budget portion. Then, the president is to work with the trustees to add their 35 percent to the budget.

(Paragraph 9) Expenditures

Budgeted amounts are not to be considered actual moneys available. The president can only spend actual funds that are available, and those moneys are to be spent according to the budget. The president may not borrow money, sign leases, buy or sell real estate, or make any agreements that could force indebtedness upon the church. Should the church borrow, the trustees may give the president authority to spend those moneys on the project for which the funds were borrowed. All undesignated moneys available to the Corporation above budgeted amounts are deemed discretionary and are available to be spent by the president, but he may only obligate funds currently on hand.

17. This section emphasizes the senior pastor's role as the spiritual leader of the local church. It distinguishes the two branches that must work in harmony—the Corporation and the spiritual Body. Then it clarifies that (a) the Corporation exists to serve the spiritual Body, and (b) that the senior pastor is responsible for leading the spiritual Body and using his influence to cause the corporate structure to serve that Body. So Section 1 emphasizes the role of senior pastor, and Section 2 explains the senior pastor's role as president of the Corporation.

18. The distinct role as president in contrast to pastor is significant. Remember that churches worship God, communicate the Word, pray for people, minister the life of the Holy Spirit to others and foster additional ministry. Corporations, on the other hand, hire and fire people, pay taxes, process money, buy and sell buildings, accumulate assets, etc. These two roles are distinctly different, but they overlap in every ministry. These Bylaws distinguish the two roles. And, as you can see, the corporate roles, when implemented with simplicity, facilitate ministry.

The Corporation, though, is not the purpose of the organization—the spiritual Body is.

So this section explains the corporate role of the senior pastor. As we have already seen, the trustees make the major financial decisions for the church. But in Paragraph 2, we notice that the pastor nominates trustees, the elders approve the nominations, and, if necessary, the pastor removes trustees. But the pastor cannot dismiss trustees at a rate faster than one every six months. This provision is needed in case the pastor's heart becomes sinful and he wants to "stack the board." Also, if the pastor has a conflict with the trustees, he can't do too much too quickly, thus everyone is protected. Remember, we want churches that remain strong and healthy for years—generations. So, the senior pastor can change the board, but not too fast. With this time delay, it would take three and a half years to change the entire board—enough time for the condition of heart to become evident to all. At the same time, should a trustee's heart become sinful, the senior pastor has the authority to remove that person quickly.

19. This paragraph clarifies that the senior pastor is the senior administrator. When a church is small, the pastor himself will often have to do all of the administration. When a church becomes large enough to afford it, a full-time administrator should be hired to serve the day-to-day ministries of the church and report directly to the senior pastor.

20. Paragraphs 4 and 5 clarify that the senior pastor, unless he is the founding pastor, is selected by the congregation, but all other staff members are hired by the senior pastor to help him serve. Therefore, according to these Bylaws, the senior pastor is ultimately accountable to the board of overseers while the rest of the staff is ultimately accountable to the senior pastor.

"I work for the church, and the staff works for me." This causes the staff to work together in great harmony and prevents unnecessary problems with staff members who might become disgruntled and try to undermine the senior pastor.

The ability of the senior pastor to set salaries is vitally important. Many church systems allow the pastor to set salaries for everyone but himself, and allow a governing board to set the pastor's salary. Not good. This could imply that the senior pastor works for a church board. He does not. The trustees already determine the home and the value of the automobiles the church will provide for the senior pastor and his family. The same problem exists if the congregation sets pastoral salaries. The implication is too strong that the senior pastor is an employee who can be hired or fired by anyone other than the board of overseers.

Most churches have four primary classifications of workers: (1) pastoral staff; (2) salaried support staff; (3) hourly support staff and

(4) volunteers. The senior pastor must design a universal pay scale for the pastoral staff. This way he knows that his base pay, experience-credit ratio and dependent allowance will be the same as the other pastors. Therefore, if he wants to pay himself a certain amount, the other pastors will need to be paid on that same scale. (Two exceptions do exist, and we will discuss them in detail later.) This provision creates a beautiful balance, and greatly reduces any sense of unfairness in pay among the pastoral team.

Our universal pay scale has evolved throughout the years, and you may be able to develop a better one than ours. But currently, our pay scale for pastoral staff starts with a $2,000-per-month base. To that base we give credit for work experience at a ratio of three to one. For every three years of experience, we give a 10 percent compounded raise. This must be experience that has helped train for the current position and does not include years in school. Thus, if someone had 12 years of qualified experience, we would give that person 4 years credit. Compounded at 10 percent a year would equal an additional $928 per month. We also give a $65-per-month allowance for every dependent. So if the pastor is married with two children, another $195 per month would be added. In this example, the pastor's gross monthly salary would be $3,123. This figure includes the pastor's housing allowance, which is nontaxable. In addition to salaries, the pastors are provided family medical insurance, retirement benefits and paid vacation. Even though this isn't an official agreement, we give at least a 10 percent raise to everyone if the church has grown 10 percent or more, which means that every person who has ever worked at New Life has received at least a 10 percent raise every year for 13 years now.

If this pay package is not enough, it is increased for all the pastoral staff. If the senior pastor can't live on the allotted amount, then the youth pastor can't either. This system has remarkable secondary benefits to the entire staff and church. For those who use it, it works very well.

Everyone would agree that the senior pastor is worthy of his hire because of his calling. Why, then, would we think a youth pastor or an administrative pastor should be paid less? If these pastors are fulfilling their callings, and God has placed them in their positions, shouldn't they also be compensated appropriately? How many youth pastors have had to become senior pastors because as their families grew, they needed to increase the family income? What a crime. Who would dare say the senior pastor works harder or longer hours than the youth pastor? No one who has been one.

The primary differential for income among the pastors should be in regard to tenure. If a pastor serves in a church for a longer period of time, that pastor will know more people and have been proven worthy of influence in more people's lives. His pay, therefore, should be raised to reflect his extended time of service. Not everyone at New Life makes the same, but all pastors are paid from the same scale.

21. The following exceptions are the only differences between the associate pastoral staff and the senior pastor, with the reasoning that the senior pastor holds corporate and spiritual responsibilities. The associate pastors and the support staff work exclusively under the senior pastor. The values of these extra benefits, though, are solely at the discretion of the trustees and outside the direct control of the senior pastor.

The two exceptions to the pay-scale system are clearly stated in Paragraph 6. Note, though, the balance in selecting the house and the vehicle(s). The trustees select the house the church will provide, so regardless of church size, if the church hires a full-time pastor, it can determine the value of the housing for the pastor and his family. In addition, the trustees determine the value of the cars the pastor receives.

If a car is wrecked during the six years, the pastor may use the remaining value in the car to replace it from insurance. These two paragraphs are very sensitive and, of course, may be changed. Some pastors already have their own homes, others prefer driving their own cars. In those cases, adjustments need to be made in this provision. For example, the trustees may choose to allow the pastor to use the financial allowance to increase his retirement. Whatever the case, make sure the senior pastor is on the same pay scale as other pastors, and that these two exceptions are not stumbling blocks.

People on the support staff are also fulfilling God's call by serving throughout the church. Support-staff pay scales are set according to job classifications, experience, responsibility, performance, etc. All of our pay rates are usually fair and in compliance with good stewardship of the tithes and offerings entrusted to us.

The view we hold regarding wage is: It is impossible to place a value on a calling. We could never afford to pay people what they are worth. So, paychecks are given to our staff out of the tithes and offerings to enable their ministries. If the church did not pay the staff, these people would have to work elsewhere to earn a living. This would greatly affect the amount of time and energy they would have available to answer their calls to ministry. Therefore, our wages are a gift, not compensation for services rendered. Hopefully, all of our staff believes so much in their callings versus their jobs, that if it were impossible for the church to pay them, they would find a way to make a living and still dedicate themselves to fulfill their callings through the church.

That brings us to volunteers. Without volunteers we could not continue to minister as effectively as we do. The fact that volunteers don't get paid does not mean they are not called. On the contrary. Volunteers themselves have clearly settled in their hearts that what they are doing is not a job. There is no hireling mentality among volunteers.

Volunteers are as much a part of the team as any paid staff member and should be treated with respect. Volunteers must be as carefully screened as staff members. You don't want to discourage good people, but trouble can occur when the volunteer process is too loose. Whether paid or not, you want the people God has called and added to your ministry team.

22. This paragraph is packed full of philosophical positions we believe are vital to protect good Christian people from overzealous leadership. Note: Budgets are prepared based on 90 percent of the previous year's unrestricted income. Why? So believers won't be constantly pressured by the church leadership to come up with extra money to meet a budget.

Too many books, tapes and videos are available on how to extract money from Christians. We receive "Christian stewardship" magazines regularly that, in essence, are teaching Christian leaders how to get money from the Body of Christ. Currently, one of the most popular speakers to the Christian-leadership world operates a for-profit ministry and is known to be extremely effective at raising money.

What's wrong with this? Christian people should be able to work, raise their families, pay their tithes to their local churches and trust that the churches are run well enough and disciplined enough to operate within their budgets. Then, if additional money comes in, that money can be used above and beyond the budgeted amounts.

In this 90-percent budget plan, even if the church income is the same as the previous year, the pastor will have 10 percent discretionary spending. If the church grows at least 10 percent, the pastor will have 20 percent discretionary spending. In 1997, New Life grew 24 percent. Therefore, we had 34 percent more income than our monthly budget, which provided flexibility toward debt reduction, missions, savings, etc. This provides great freedom for all!

In the preparation of the budget, the senior pastor has available 65 percent of the 90 percent figure. He meets with the trustees to offer his suggestions for the remaining 35 percent. We suggest the senior pastor have a proposal prepared and then, with the wisdom of the trustees, set the budget for the upcoming year. Budgeting should be done annually.

We don't publish our budgets. They are in-house documents that give our Administration Department direction for allocations to all departments. We only publish our cash-flow statements at year-end and make our audit reports available to the public—although within the past 12 years, no one has ever requested our audit reports.

ARTICLE EIGHT

Overseers[23]

(**Paragraph 1**) [church name] Requirements for
   Overseers
The members of the board of overseers must be
active senior pastors of respected congregations who
know and love [church name] and the pastor. They
must agree to make themselves available at their own
expense to serve [church name] if requested by the
elders (Article Thirteen, Section 2), and must be willing to provide spiritual protection to the church
through prayer and by exemplifying honorable
Christian lives.

(**Paragraph 2**) Biblical Qualifications for Overseers
"Now the overseer must be above reproach, the
husband of but one wife, temperate, self-controlled, respectable, hospitable, able to teach, not
given to drunkenness, not violent but gentle, not
quarrelsome, not a lover of money. He must manage
his own family well and see that his children obey
him with proper respect. (If anyone does not know
how to manage his own family, how can he take
care of God's church?) He must not be a recent convert, or he may become conceited and fall under
the same judgment as the devil. He must also have
a good reputation with outsiders, so that he will
not fall into disgrace and into the devil's trap"
(1 Tim. 3:2-7).

(**Paragraph 3**) Selection and Function of Overseers
A board of overseers will be nominated by the pastor

and confirmed by the elders. The pastor will be accountable to the overseers in the event of alleged misconduct in compliance with Article Thirteen.

(Paragraph 4) Installing New Overseers
The senior pastor and the elders may replace overseers at the rate of one per year and enter that change into the minutes of a trustees meeting. If disciplinary action is being considered, changes in the board of overseers may not be made until its work is completed.

23. This provision is unique for independent churches. Here, an outside board is given authority to discipline the senior pastor. These Bylaws allow checks and balances to all leadership groups. Additional details are given in Article Nine.

Members of the overseers must be pastors of local churches that know and love your local church and the pastor. They must be pastors who would make themselves available at their own expense to your church to help during difficult times. This provision is vitally important for the security of an independent church, resulting in its greater health and success. When believers in an independent church know that their pastor can be disciplined or fired, they are willing to place greater trust in him.

ARTICLE NINE

Elders[24]

(Paragraph 1) Spiritual Role
The elders are to serve the congregation and the senior pastor for the development of the spiritual life of the church. These people and their spouses are to help create a positive spiritual climate within the church Body. They are neither a governing or corporate board, but a spiritual body called to create and maintain stability in potentially negative situations.

(Paragraph 2) Definition
The elders are people who function within the local church but are not members of the pastoral staff of the church. They meet the biblical qualifications for eldership and function in that calling, but derive their income from sources other than the church. The number of elders shall be determined by the senior pastor but shall not be less than 12.

(Paragraph 3) Functions[25]
The functions of the elders are to:

1. Maintain and teach by living a godly, Christian lifestyle;
2. Provide a prayer shield for the pastoral team and the local church;
3. Defend, protect and support the integrity of the pastoral team and the local church;
4. Pray for the sick;
5. Organize, implement and execute licensing and ordination requirements and procedures;
6. Mediate disputes among the brethren;
7. Counsel;
8. Confirm or reject pastoral appointments to the board of trustees and the board of overseers;
9. Contact the board of overseers to initiate investigation and potential discipline of the senior pastor;
10. Represent the church to other local churches.

(Paragraph 4) Biblical Qualification for Eldership
"An elder must be blameless, the husband of but one wife, a man whose children believe and are not open to the charge of being wild and disobedient. Since an

overseer is entrusted with God's work, he must be blameless—not overbearing, not quick-tempered, not given to drunkenness, not violent, not pursuing dishonest gain. Rather he must be hospitable; one who loves what is good, who is self-controlled, upright, holy and disciplined. He must hold firmly to the trustworthy message as it has been taught, so that he can encourage others by sound doctrine and refute those who oppose it" (Titus 1:6-9).

(Paragraph 5) Nomination and Appointment to the Board of Elders[26]
Selection of the elders will be preceded by the senior pastor's teaching on the biblical requirements for eldership at a Sunday service. Each adult present at the service will make one anonymous nomination for the position of elder in writing immediately after the sermon on eldership. The pastor and his associates will tally these nominations, and the elders will be selected from those with the largest number of nominations. The senior pastor can veto anyone's nomination. This nomination process should occur once every four years unless needed to add additional elders to complete a four-year cycle.

(Paragraph 6) Four-Year-Service Terms
Once selected to serve on the elder board, the elder and spouse are to serve for four years. After that time of service, the selection process is to be repeated and anyone renominated and appointed may serve as many times as the congregation and pastor choose. However, should the congregation fail to renominate any certain elder, the pastor may not select that person for service.

(Paragraph 7) Removal of an Elder

Should anyone in the congregation, including a staff member or another elder, bring accusation against an elder, charging that the person does not qualify for eldership, a seven-member group from the staff and the elder board may hear the accusations and any response from the accused elder. Three of the seven-member group are to be chosen by the accused elder, and four are to be chosen by the senior pastor. The senior pastor may not serve on the panel judging the elder, but may oversee the procedures if he chooses. Then, in an anonymous vote, if five or more agree that the elder does not meet the qualifications for eldership, that elder may no longer serve on the elder board.

(Paragraph 8) Replacement of Elders

During the four years of service, those elders who are no longer able to serve for any reason need not be replaced unless the total number of elders is decreased to less than twelve.

24. This is the only "board" that includes the spouses in its function. All elders meetings and functions should fully include the spouses because of the function they have within the Body. We see the elders as the rudder on the bottom of the boat—keeping it upright in the midst of a storm. We also see the elders as the primary prayer shield for the church.

25. The ten functions of the elders are listed in the Bylaws for a specific reason. The elders do not have the same responsibilities as the trustees—even though from time to time they may want to—nor do they have the same responsibilities as the overseers. They are, instead, colaborers with the senior pastor and his staff to fulfill the spiritual direction and calling of the church.

26. This paragraph explains the process for selecting elders. We think it's best not to announce when this service will take place so lobbying does not occur. You want an honest, impromptu response from the congregation. Here's how to do it: The senior pastor should preach about the qualifications for an elder. Then have the ushers hand out three-by-five

cards and ask the congregation to clearly write the name of one person in the church who most fits the qualifications of an elder. Read the Bible text one more time while people are thinking and writing. Have the ushers pick up all the cards and give them to a member of the pastoral team.

At that point, no one knows if they were nominated or how many times. It's important that the senior pastor's office tally the nominations confidentially. During the sorting process, some people may need to be disqualified by the pastoral team. Because of the nature of their positions, they will know about some people in the congregation who will be nominated who, in fact, should not serve as elders for personal reasons. Those facts should not be made known to anyone.

Then you can create a list of potential elders. Send the select nominees letters explaining that they have been nominated as elders. Include the scriptural basis for eldership and delineate the 10 eldership responsibilities (like a job description). Ask the nominees to evaluate their own lives to see if they think they qualify to serve for a four-year term.

Should they need to decline, they do not have to give a reason. Should they accept, they should call the office and let you know. That group and their spouses may serve for four years. Schedule a time during a Sunday service to recognize and commission the new elders and their spouses. Explain briefly the responsibilities of elders and have the congregation pray over them.

We suggest that if an elder develops difficulties, that person not be removed from office too quickly. There may be exceptions, and thus the provision in Paragraph 7. When elders face difficulty in their families or personal lives, they will usually resign. However, if the board is large enough to absorb the temporary unavailability of an elder(s) working through personal conflict, the benefits gained will outweigh removing the person(s). It is best to stay in the tree of life in these groups as much as possible. Relax and be full of grace.

ARTICLE TEN

Officers

Section 1. Officers[27]

The officers of the Corporation shall be a president and a secretary/treasurer and any other officers that the trustees may authorize from time to time.

Section 2. Appointment, Election and Term of Office

(Paragraph 1) Appointment of the President
The appointment responsibilities of the president are listed in Articles Five and Seven.

(Paragraph 2) Appointment of Secretary/Treasurer
The secretary-treasurer is to be nominated by the president and approved by the trustees. The term of this office is indefinite. Should the trustees fail to approve of the nomination from the president, other nominations must be made until a candidate suitable to the trustees is nominated. The president may remove the secretary/treasurer.

(Paragraph 3) New Offices
New offices may be created and filled at any meeting of the board of trustees. Each officer shall hold office until his successor has been duly elected and qualified.

Section 3. Removal of Officers

(Paragraph 1) Overseers' Responsibility for the President
The overseers of the church may discipline or remove the president according to Article Thirteen.

(Paragraph 2) Trustees' Responsibility for All Other Officers
Any officer elected or appointed by the board of trustees may be removed by the board when the best interests of the Corporation would be served thereby, but such removal shall be without prejudice to the contract rights, if any, of the officer so removed.

Section 4. Powers of Officers

(Paragraph 1) The President
The powers of the president are listed in Article Seven.

(Paragraph 2) The Secretary/Treasurer
As secretary, the secretary/treasurer shall attend all sessions of the board of trustees, and shall act as clerk thereof to record (or have recorded) all votes and the minutes of all proceedings in a book to be kept for that purpose. This person shall oversee the keeping of the membership rolls of the Corporation, and in general perform the duties usually incident to the office of secretary, and such further duties as shall be prescribed from time to time by the board of trustees or by the president.

(Paragraph 3) The Secretary/Treasurer's Role over Accounting
As treasurer, the secretary/treasurer shall oversee the keeping of full and accurate accounts of the receipts and disbursements in books belonging to the Corporation. The secretary/treasurer shall also oversee the deposit of all moneys and other valuable effects in the name and to the credit of the Corporation in such banks and depositories as may be designated by the president. The secretary/treasurer does not determine expenditures, but does oversee the disbursement of the funds of the Corporation as may be ordered by the trustees or the president. This person shall perform the duties usually incident to the office of treasurer and such other duties as may be prescribed from time to time by the board of trustees or by the president.[28]

(Paragraph 4) Audited Financial Statements

The secretary/treasurer shall serve on the Audit Review Committee and report to the trustees after its review of the annual audit. If the church does not have an annual audit, the secretary/treasurer is to provide to the board a report on the previous year's income and disbursements.

(Paragraph 5) Cash Flow Statements

The secretary/treasurer is to work with the president to provide an annual cash flow statement that must accompany all giving receipts to members. That report is to include the specific amounts of cash remuneration received from the church to specific pastoral staff members. Benefits, support staff salaries and other items may be grouped together, but the cash portion of the pastoral pay packages must be itemized individually.[29]

(Paragraph 6) Public Availability of Annual Financial Statements

The secretary/treasurer shall insure that current audited financial statements are available to anyone upon written request, and that the previous year's cash flow statements are available to all contributors to the church.

Section 5. Trustees' Selection of Additional Officers[30]

In the absence of any officer of the Corporation, except the president, or for any other reason that may seem necessary to the board, the board of trustees, by a majority vote, may delegate the duties and powers of that officer for the time being to any other officer, or to any trustee.

27. In Colorado, the law requires only two officers. Check your own state law to see what is required. Avoid having vice presidents, because the

implication is that the vice president will become president should the president no longer be in the church. And this is not true. If three officers are required by your state, I suggest appointing a president/pastor, secretary and treasurer. However, if possible, combine the secretary/treasurer position.

The secretary/treasurer is appointed by the president and approved by the board of trustees. That appointment is permanent unless the person resigns or is removed by the president.

28. There is a subtle safety measure here that some don't catch. The secretary/treasurer is responsible to oversee the bookkeeping of the church. The secretary/treasurer is not responsible to determine expenditures, but is responsible to make sure accurate records are being kept and reported. The financial office does our bookkeeping. The financial office works under the senior pastor but is also accountable to the secretary/treasurer.

Why is that important? Because if the senior pastor became dishonest or began to do something unusual with finances, the accounting staff would be responsible to tell him without any fear of recourse. If he did not correct the situation, they would then bring it to the attention of the secretary/treasurer. A safety measure such as this protects the pastor from a greedy, deceptive heart, and protects the accounting staff in the midst of a potentially difficult situation. It is very important that someone not paid by the church oversees the financial records. This system works very well.

The provision's requirement that the secretary/treasurer attend all sessions of the board of trustees does not mean the board cannot meet and do business when the secretary/treasurer is absent. It means the secretary/treasurer's functions must be performed when the secretary/treasurer is absent, and that if the secretary/treasurer is in town, every effort must be made on this person's part to attend.

29. This paragraph is vitally important. We believe that everyone who gives to the church should be able to know exactly how much money the church received, how much was spent and for what (i.e., each pastoral staff member's salary on a line-item basis). Believing that the funds given to the church are people's worship to God and knowing that cash-flow statements must be mailed out at the end of every year makes those who spend the tithes and offerings much more thoughtful. They know that the missions support, internal payroll, benevolence gifts, operations expenses and other expenditures will be openly accounted for and not "hidden" in a pie chart or percentage graph.

30. Section Five allows for additional officers. I don't recommend this because I think every circumstance should be covered with the already

existing provisions. However, if something unforeseen develops, this provision does allow flexibility.

ARTICLE ELEVEN

Business Practices
Section 1. Fiscal Year
The fiscal year of the Corporation shall be the calendar year.
Section 2. Contracts
The board of trustees may authorize any officer or officers, agent or agents of the Corporation, in addition to the officers so authorized by these Bylaws, to enter into any contract or execute and deliver any instrument in the name of and on behalf of the Corporation. Such authority may be general or may be confined to specific instances.
Section 3. Checks, Drafts or Orders
All checks, drafts, orders for the payment of money, notes or other evidences of indebtedness issued in the name of the Corporation shall be signed by such officer or officers, agent or agents of the Corporation, and in such manner, as shall from time to time be determined by resolution of the board of trustees. In the absence of such determination by the board of trustees, such instruments may be signed by either the secretary/treasurer or the president of the Corporation in accordance with their duties outlined in these Bylaws.
Section 4. Deposits
All funds of the Corporation shall be deposited to the credit of the Corporation in such banks, trust companies or other depositories as the board of trustees may select in accordance with these Bylaws.
Section 5. Gifts
The president/pastor may accept on behalf of the Corporation any contribution, gift, bequest or device for any purpose of the Corporation.
Section 6. Books and Records
The Corporation shall keep correct and complete books and records of account. The Corporation shall also keep minutes of the

proceedings of its members, board of trustees, committees having and exercising any of the authority of the board of trustees and any other committees. It shall keep at the principal office a record giving the names and addresses of all board members entitled to vote.

ARTICLE TWELVE

Church Ministry
Section 1. Minister Ordination and Licensing

(Paragraph 1) Role of the Board of Elders
The elders may ordain and/or license a person as a minister of the gospel after first examining the applicant's background, moral and religious character, and previous Bible courses and/or independent studies completed. Final determination shall be within the absolute discretion of the board of elders.

(Paragraph 2) Application Through the Board of Elders
Application for ordination and/or licensing as a minister of the gospel shall be supplied on the form provided by the elders. An application shall be either approved or denied within 90 days of the completion of the investigation of the applicant by the board of elders. Those applicants who are approved shall receive a certificate evidencing the approval.

(Paragraph 3) Ability to Limit Ministry Validation
The spiritual leadership of the church may at its own discretion limit any licensee ordained to an area of special emphasis.

Section 2. Ministry Training
The senior pastor and his staff may establish a School of Ministry,

setting forth a prescribed curriculum and course of study leading to ordination and licensing of ministers. The School of Ministry shall prepare students in the knowledge of the Word of God and in ministering to people's needs through the gospel of Jesus Christ.

ARTICLE THIRTEEN

Church Discipline
Section 1. Disciplining Church Members[31]

Only members are subject to church discipline.

Section 2. Disciplining the Pastor[32]

(Paragraph 1) Criteria for Discipline
Should the senior pastor demonstrate immoral conduct, financial practices or theological views, which the majority of the elders believe may require either personal correction or termination of his position, the elders shall contact the senior pastor and then, if the problem remains, be the overseers for investigation and evaluation of any appropriate discipline. (See Article Nine, Paragraph 3.)

(Paragraph 2) Process for Investigation
Should the overseers be asked to investigate alleged pastoral misconduct, a consensus of three of the five overseers is required to take disciplinary action. With such a consensus, the overseers shall assume complete authority over the senior pastor. They may decide to remove him from his position or to discipline him in any way they deem necessary. The overseers have no authority in [church name] unless contacted by the elders, and then only insofar as permitted under these Bylaws.

[266]

(Paragraph 3) Motivation
It is the intention of the Corporation to protect the hearts of all involved in matters of pastoral discipline. Using the method outlined in these Bylaws, the "sheep" never have to pass judgment upon their "shepherd."

31. This section provides for those occasions when the spiritual leadership of the Body needs to discipline a member of the congregation. Because worship services are open to anyone, the opportunity for church discipline is limited to those who are members in accordance with Article Two. Thus, an immoral or dishonest member may be disciplined. There is a biblical requirement for this function, and it simply provides a legal limitation of who would be protected by practical church oversight.

32. The disciplinary procedures in this section can be applied in one of three situations:
    - *Questionable moral conduct* such as elicit sexual activities, etc.
    - *Questionable financial practices* such as stealing money, tax fraud or some type of intentional dishonest activity with church or personal funds, properties or assets, which also includes a flagrant lack of good judgment in personal business decisions and/or allowing business schemes to affect the church fund-raising, causing harm to the spiritual life of the church.
    - *Questionable theological views* the pastor believes and teaches that are contrary to the theological views outlined in Article Three. This is to protect the church from heresy.

    The senior pastor should never be disciplined for simple personal preferences. Decisions such as guest-speaker selection (unless the speaker is invited to teach a heresy with the support of the senior pastor), scheduling services, selection of carpet color or anything purely subjective are not the bases for pastoral discipline. Sound judgment is to be evaluated before he is given the position of senior pastor. Once in office, the senior pastor can only be questioned and disciplined for a major mistake as outlined in Article Nine. This guarantees him freedom to boldly lead the spiritual Body of believers.

    This section also provides a benefit that is usually found only in denominational churches. It prevents the congregation, board or church members from having to judge or even talk about the discipline of their own senior pastor. Your Bylaws or minutes of a board meeting should include a current list of five overseers who know the church and the senior pastor. All five overseers should currently be pastors of local churches, and should be respected by your church and your senior pastor. These overseers have full authority, once contacted by an elder. Contacting the overseers is the only way within the church to discipline a senior pastor.

ARTICLE FOURTEEN

Amendment of Bylaws[33]

These Bylaws may be altered, amended or repealed, and new Bylaws may be adopted, by a five-to-seven (5/7) vote of the board of trustees at any regular board meeting. At least five days advance written notice of said meeting shall be given to each member of the board. The written notice must explain proposed changes. These Bylaws may also be altered, amended or repealed, and new Bylaws may be adopted by consent in writing signed by all members of the board of trustees.

Bylaws were approved by the board of trustees of [church name] on [date].

[Attach names of officers and trustees.]

33. This provision is for the amendment of the Bylaws of the church, but only under extreme circumstances. Notice that written notice of such changes must be made five days in advance and that the majority (five to seven) of the trustees must agree. This is the only time a quorum does not have the authority to take official action.

The information in this chapter should give you a starting point. Remember, take what will prove useful to you and discard the rest. We think it works well as a package and has philosophical continuity. However, each church is unique and state laws do differ.

Now you have a strong philosophical basis for a life-giving church. In addition, you have a brief overview of some of the ministries and a foundation for the business of the church. The foundation is ready, now let's give life together.

BLESSED ARE THOSE WHO WASH THEIR ROBES, THAT
THEY MAY HAVE THE RIGHT TO THE TREE OF LIFE
AND MAY GO THROUGH THE GATES INTO THE CITY.

[Revelation 22:14]

Fill Your Church With New Life

From Barrenness to Fruitfulness
Frank Damazio
How God Can Use You to Birth New Life in Your Church

Hardcover
ISBN 08307.23374

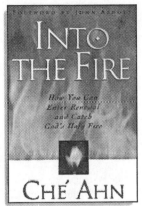

Into the Fire
Ché Ahn
How You Can Enter Renewal and Catch God's Holy Fire

Hardcover
ISBN 08307.23439

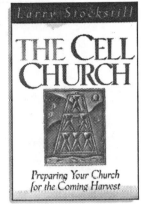

The Cell Church
Larry Stockstill
A Model for Ministering to Every Member of the Body of Christ

Hardcover
ISBN 08307.20723

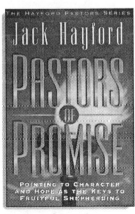

Pastors of Promise
Jack Hayford
Pointing to Character and Hope as the Keys to Fruitful Shepherding

Paperback
ISBN 08307.18079

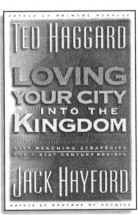

Loving Your City Into the Kingdom
Ted Haggard
City-Reaching Strategies for a 21st Century Revival

Paperback
ISBN 08307.18958
Video • UPC 607135.001119

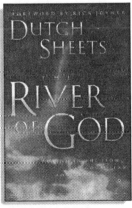

The River of God
Dutch Sheets
Moving in the Flow of God's Plan for Revival

Hardcover
ISBN 08307.20731

Available at your local Christian bookstore.

Great Ways to Keep Churches Growing

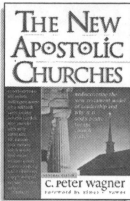

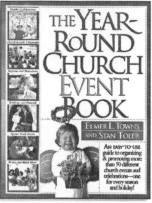
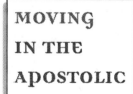

PLAN NOW TO ATTEND THE

Life-Giving Leadership

CONFERENCE

THE FIRST WEEK OF JUNE EVERY YEAR

If you're involved in church leadership of any kind, this conference is for you! Join Pastor Ted Haggard at New Life Church in Colorado Springs to be refreshed, refined and refocused!

TEACHING
Each morning a different keynote speakers will address real life issues that you deal with every day as a leader.

WORKSHOPS
The main teaching sessions are complemented with practical, Q&A-style workshops, led by a variety of speakers. Topics Include:

- Breaking Habitual Sin Patterns
- Personal Purity—Sex
- Empowering Relationships
- Easy Church Government That Works
- Deliverance
- Personal Freedom
- Restoring Broken Relationships
- How to Become a Cell Church
- Life-giving Church Structure
- Praise and Worship

- Assimilating Visitors
- Money Management
- How to Be the Wife of a Ministry Leader
- Youth Ministries—Staff Relationships
- Elder/Deacon Roles and Relationships
- The Ministry of Administration
- Strategic Global Outreach
- How to Train Leaders
- Media Systems and Communication
- *AND MORE*

Gospel Light

This Conference is held at New Life Church, 11025 State Hwy 83 North, Colorado Springs, CO 80921. For additional information call (719) 594-6602

CITY-REACHING STRATEGIES
For The 21st Century Revival

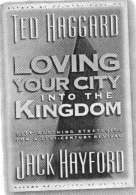

LOVING YOUR CITY INTO THE KINGDOM
Catch the Vision of Reaching Your City for Christ
by Ted Haggard & Jack Hayford

This resource guide is a must for your library. This book contains some of the best material from 23 of the most respected authorities on church growth, worldwide evangelism, prayer, spiritual mapping, church relationships, revival and city-reaching strategies.

Ted Haggard
Four steps to impact our cities: Praying together, Planning together, Going together, Growing together.

Jack Hayford
How to pray against the destruction of our cities.

Dr. Bill Bright
Fasting for Revival.

Dr. C. Peter Wagner
Five essentials for effective spiritual warfare.

Ed Silvoso
Prayer Evangelism.

Steve Hawthorne
Prayerwalking: Praying On-site with Insight Saturating your city with prayer.

George Barna
You need information.

George Otis, Jr.
Spiritual Mapping.

Don Argue
Relationships to Other Christian Denominations: Diverse Body, One Message.

AND MANY MORE!

Hardcover available for $15
Softcover available for $12

LOVING YOUR CITY INTO THE KINGDOM VIDEO SEMINAR
Share the Vision of Reaching Your City for Christ
by Ted Haggard

Based on the books *Primary Purpose* and *Loving Your City into the Kingdom* this video seminar outlines proven principles and lifestyle guidelines for uniting Christians in effective city-wide outreach to the lost. But most of all, this seminar will help you mobilize your congregation by revealing God's heart for reaching unbelievers. Show it in your Small Group meetings, Sunday School classes or to your congregation and watch them be inspired to reach out in love!
2 video set - 200 minutes in approximately 1 1/2 hour teaching sessions. $ 32

PRIMARY PURPOSE
Making It Hard for People to Go to Hell From Your City
by Ted Haggard

You can change your city's spiritual climate. *Primary Purpose* contains practical principles and inspirational insights on how believers can impact their communities for Christ.
Softcover available for $10